A Sunset Book

Furniture Finishing
and Refinishing

By James B. Johnstone
and the Sunset Editorial Staff

Lane Books · Menlo Park, California

Foreword

Few homes are without one or more pieces of furniture that the owner would like to see refinished. However, the relatively high cost of commercial finishing, or the natural hesitancy to tackle an unfamiliar job without guidance, usually condemns the pieces to remaining as-is or being discarded. This book provides answers to most finishing needs, from quick cover-ups to the finest traditional surfaces. Fast and serviceable finishes, fine finishes, and the more useful of the decorative finishes are presented.

The creative aspects of do-it-yourself finishing are every bit as important as those related to economics. The amateur can take the time to achieve exact colors, finishes, and textures, and to perform experiments with materials, color, and texture that he might hesitate to ask or pay for from a professional. Anyone can produce highly acceptable first finishing jobs with minimal equipment simply by following the common sense procedures given in this book. With a little practice, finishes equal or superior to commercial ones are possible.

Well built, unfinished furniture made with cabinet woods deserves the very best modern or traditional finishes. Less expensive unfinished furniture may need only the quick, attractive cover-ups listed in the chapter on unfinished furniture. Highly individual hand detailing touches that provide interesting highlights and accents but which are too often omitted for lack of handy reference materials are covered in the chapter on decorative finishes, which details glazing, antiquing, decoupage, gilding, stenciling, striping, and flocking.

We acknowledge with gratitude the aid of many individuals who made their furniture, materials, time, and experience available in the preparation of this book. The fine antique corner cupboard shown in the cover photograph was provided by Mary F. Rafferty, Antiques, Menlo Park, California.

PHOTOGRAPHS by James B. Johnstone except the following:
Glenn M. Christiansen: Cover, pages 20, 56, 59, 61 (bottom). Martha Rosman: page 52.
Darrow M. Watt: pages 61 (top, center), 63 (right), 74.

ILLUSTRATIONS by Dinah James.

Executive Editor, Sunset Books: David E. Clark

Tenth Printing April 1974

Contents

SPECIAL FEATURES

Introduction

Wood finishing has held an honored place among the crafts for many centuries. Decorative earth and vegetable colors were used long before the first wood finishes appeared in Egypt and surrounding regions between 1500 and 1000 B.C.

Furniture and other wooden objects, for example, found in Egyptian tombs show the use of polychrome decoration, bituminous coatings, and fossil vegetable gum, clear varnishes (notably amber). Some of the fossil and vegetable gum spirit varnishes known in ancient and medieval times are still in limited use: dammar varnish is used by artists as a protective and a fixative; and copal is used as an extender or adulterant in shellac and varnish substitutes.

Shellac

The major spirit varnish used today is shellac. The shell-like exudate of an insect, the lac bug, native to India, is left as scale encrusted on twigs of host trees. The scale is collected and the lac resin removed, cleaned, graded, processed and shipped as light amber flakes or buttons of pure shellac. Strangely, this most frequently used of the natural finishing resins has been known for over 2,000 years. Originally, the bugs were cultivated for the dye produced and the lac resin was considered a waste product. The lac itself was used in India about 1600 A.D., and shellac became an industrial staple during the 19th century in Europe for the production of fine finishes. The refined lac resin became known as "shell-lac" or "shellac."

Shellac is normally supplied in two forms, orange and white. The orange shellac can vary from deep orange to a medium amber in color. The white shellac, as in water "white," is simply a purified and bleached version of orange shellac.

An extra-high-quality white shellac is sometimes available at art supply houses as French varnish.

Varnish

In spite of the excellent finish possible with shellac, it is not durable in the presence of moisture, alkaline solutions, alcohols and many other solvents. A search to find a shellac substitute with improved durability resulted in the production of modern oleoresinous varnishes and lacquers. Oleoresinous varnishes are combinations of drying oils and natural resins which produce durable, glossy surfaces but are considered too slow-drying for industrial use without investing in large drying equipment.

Varnish ingredients have, over the years, shifted almost entirely from natural resins to improved synthetic resins.

Lacquer

Cellulose nitrate lacquers became available in quantity after World War I. While more durable than shellac, the lacquers were at first naturally dull and had to be rubbed to a gloss. With the production of good glossy synthetic lacquers, industry largely abandoned shellac and varnish for furniture finishing.

Penetrating Resin

Penetrating resin finishes for wood were introduced as penetrating floor finishes and gained popularity with the introduction of Scandinavian furniture styles in the 1950's. These resin finishes are really research byproducts of synthetic varnish and lacquer production techniques.

A major contribution of the Orient was the discovery, sometime between 200 and 500 A.D., that sap from certain "lacquer" or "varnish" trees could be cured to make durable, hard, waterproof "lacquer." It is actually an exotic varnish rather than a lacquer in the modern sense, but it is called "lacquer" by tradition.

Oriental lacquer cures best in a moist atmosphere, rather than in the warm, dry air required for most finishes. In fact, Oriental lacquer is often cured in moist caves or cellars. The Oriental lacquer process, with later refinements of bright colors and metallic leafing, produced the fine lacquer finishes introduced to the Western World by Marco Polo and his contemporaries.

Trade with China in the seventeenth and eighteenth centuries and Perry's opening of Japan to the Western world in 1834 provided the inspiration for "French Polish" in France and England in an attempt to compete with the Oriental lacquer finishes.

The development of the oleoresinous varnishes and modern lacquers finally allowed Western finishes to equal the durability of the Oriental finishes.

Processes involved in the producing and application of finishing materials have remained fundamentally the same over many centuries, with some refinement and simplification. Some examples are garnet and synthetic abrasives used in place of river sand or shark's skin, and brushes or spray guns used in place of feathers, rabbits' feet or squirrel tails.

The real differences lie in the modern finishes themselves. Modern chemistry has, for all practical purposes, rebuilt the finishing industry. Modern finishes are generally more beautiful and, for the most part, easier to produce.

The craftsman should start fresh when considering furniture finishing. He should follow the step-by-step instructions that accompany modern finishing products. Once proficient in the recommended techniques, there is ample time to experiment with other techniques.

In this book you may find an occasional variation from a manufacturer's recommendations, but in the circumstance given, the variation is believed to be justified. If you suspect that there may be a difference between the example given in the book and the product you have purchased, experiment with small quantities of the product on scrap wood. The test wood pieces should be carefully marked with information on abrasive grades, stain, sealer, finish and rubbing procedures, and stored for future reference.

A few trade terms are used in this book to help you when purchasing finishing materials at a paint or hardware store. When you are not certain of a particular trade term, *refer to the glossary* for clarification.

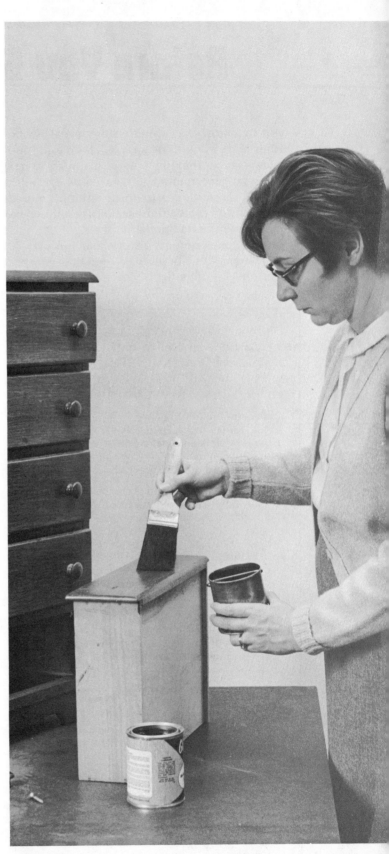

VARNISHING *over a grained glaze surface gives handsome finish to old chest of drawers (see page 48).*

Before You Start the Job...

A visit to almost any furniture store reveals wood finishes in an astonishing array of color, tone, and surface texture. There may be as many as 30 oak finishes, ranging from a light, grayed-wheat finish with high gloss surface to "high fashion," muted green, red, and brown finishes. Between these extremes lie all the traditional finishes.

For example, walnut is also available in over 30 combinations of color and texture. Other finishes range from the ultra-light, bleached, smooth surfaces to the highly textured, "ship's timbers" surfaces. And there is, generally, no absence of provincial, traditional, and conservative modern finishes. Mahogany, birch, and maple finishes display a similar variety.

It is interesting to note that only some furniture finishes are mechanically identical in color and texture from piece to piece. The more expensive furniture will have varying finishes as a result of individual treatment that brings out the best qualities

Table 1
TYPE OF FINISH DESIRED

CLEAR FINISHES

Penetrating finish. Easiest in application. Fast drying. Easy to repair. Hardens surface. "Fires" natural wood colors and grain. Similar in appearance to traditional "oil" finish. Especially good on darker woods. Best on open grain woods.

Shellac. Ease and speed of applications. Easy to repair. Rubs to satin or gloss finish. Finest of finishes for clarity and "fire." Excellent adhesion and abrasion resistance. Easily damaged or marred by alkaline solutions, moisture, alcohol, and other solvents.

Lacquer. Clear, tough finish used on most furniture since 1920's. Fast drying to allow many coats in a few hours. Rubs to satin or gloss finish. Fairly easy to repair damages on the surface. Most lacquers require spray equipment for application. Very fast drying, making it somewhat of a problem for the inexperienced finisher. Tends to be inflexible and cracks easily.

Varnish. Toughest on-the-wood finish. Fewer coats are needed for "built-up" finish. Gives warmth to wood, and color effect is similar to an oil finish, with the grain emphasized. Slow drying, and dust is a problem. Not easy to obtain a good surface without practice.

SEMI-OPAQUE FINISHES

Clear Top Coat. Pigmented wiping stain (to obscure or disguise grain) under any of the clear finishes.

Stained Top Coat. Pigment or stain added to any clear finish to give appearance of transparency while obscuring surface. (Varnish stain, lacquer stain.)

OPAQUE FINISHES

Enamel. Pigmented varnish type vehicle to completely obliterate wood character. For smooth finish and color.

Lacquer. Pigmented lacquer—usually sprayed—for smooth uniform color finish. Fast drying.

Shellac. Pigmented shellac similar to pigmented lacquer.

Table 2
IDENTIFICATION OF OLD FINISH

Shellac. Most old pre-1920 clear finishes contained shellac. Dissolves in alcohol (Denatured).*

Lacquer. Most commercial furniture after 1920. Dissolves in lacquer thinner.

Varnish and Paints. Softened by lacquer thinner or remover—lifts but does not dissolve.

Milk or Refractory Paint. Early American country pieces—rough dull paint usually black, green or red. Removes with a full-strength ammonia scrub.

*Old or adulterated shellac often becomes effectively insoluble through aging—in such a case, treat it as a varnish.

in each piece. The finishes on the best pieces are much clearer than those on the less expensive pieces.

Don't feel that the finish on each piece of furniture must be an exact duplicate of any other piece that you have finished. Within a reasonable range, any slight difference in the wood finish will add interest. A room of furniture finished in the same way may offer monotony rather than the pleasing harmony of related pieces.

If you are in doubt as to the final finish to use on any furniture finishing project, go to one or more of the furniture or antique stores in your area. Note the furniture finishes that appeal to you. You need not follow the examples exactly, but it does help to know the finishes and furniture styles that are considered worth buying.

In finishing your own furniture, any finish you choose is fine, if it pleases you. However, if you are "investing" in your refinishing project with a thought to future sale of the finished piece, consider the market carefully before applying a finish that will make it difficult to resell.

The first step in any finishing or refinishing project is to have a good idea of the finished end product (see Table 1).

Step two is to identify the old finish (see Table 2).

Step three is to decide whether any part of the present finish can be cleaned, restored, or repaired and used within your concept of the desired end product (see Table 3).

Step four is to decide whether you want a "new furniture" look or an antique look (see Table 4).

Table 3
CONDITION OF SURFACE

Dirty. If the surface is sound and of solid wood or thick veneer, scrub with detergent in water, then wipe with mineral spirits. If thin or damaged veneer, wipe with damp rag, then mineral spirits. It's surprising how often this solves a "finishing" problem, when followed by several coats of good floor wax and elbow grease.

If bare wood, try above plus alcohol, lacquer thinner or bleaches to remove dirt or stains. If they fail, sanding below dirt or stain will be necessary.

Adhesion of old finish. With handle in palm and thumb in bowl, drag edge of spoon bowl over inconspicuous section of finish, attempting to mar surface. If it merely surface mars instead of chipping or flaking off, it is there to stay if it suits your need. If it comes off, remove. A large coin or dull putty knife also works.

Chipped or gouged. If old finish is sound except for chips, burns or gouges, consider local shellac stick or putty fill and repair.

Textured. Large cracks, alligatoring, blisters, or other large finish voids that occur over large areas call for stripping and refinishing.

Fine cracks, crazing, wrinkling and similar fine textured defects in shellac or lacquer can often be repaired—with varying degrees of success—see page 71. All varnish defects that cannot be rubbed out and overcoated call for stripping and refinishing—varnish is generally hardest of all to repair, since once "set-up" it can't successfully be redissolved and blended.

Table 4
"OLD OR NEW" TREATMENT

New Wood Look (Usually not for antiques). Strip and sand for clean new surface look. Bleach if any "old" color (stain or patina) remains. Finish as for unfinished furniture.

Retain Old Color or Patina. Strip gently—layer by layer if necessary—and use only smooth round edged scrapers and absolute minimum 400 grit sanding, then refinish to retain old color tone.

SPOON DRAG TEST quickly reveals that old finish has not adhered; should be removed and refinished.

Knowing Your Woods

In any furniture finishing or refinishing, it is helpful to know a few basic facts about wood and how to identify the most commonly used furniture woods. It is also helpful to know something of the colors and treatments most often applied to these woods.

Master craftsmen of each of the great furniture periods had their favorite woods and developed many of the colors associated with those woods. Aside from the more modern materials themselves,

it is doubtful if any color or combinations of colors now in use was unknown to these master craftsmen. As with most manufacturers today, the craftsmen stayed largely with the colors of current fashion—simply because that's what sold. Someone had to be experimenting, though, or the marvelous French polishes and the pearlescent glazed golds under porcelain-ivory finishes (of Marie Antoinette fame) would never have been created.

A brief visit to one of the major museums having wooden artifacts from prehistoric and present primitive societies will reveal shapes, uses, colors and color combinations of wood that most of us consider modern. It is also interesting to note that ancient craftsmen often used several combinations of color and texture to frame or emphasize a particularly fine wood specimen.

Museum prowling and browsing through antique and fine furniture collections and stores can provide many hours of interest, enjoyment, and ideas for the refinishing projects.

Learn to recognize the woods most often used in fine and antique furniture. Notice the textures of woods and finishes, the clarity or opacity of finishes, the patterns of wear and the effects of aging. Also note the color hues and tones used and whether they appear to have been true transparent stains or pigmented paint products used as stains. A knowledge of the woods and hues most often used with specific periods or styles is helpful in making your own furniture finishing decisions, even if you should decide to depart creatively from the norms.

Wood Description

Alder, Red (*Alnus rubra*) also western alder. *Source:* Pacific coast of North America, northern California and north. *Color and pattern:* Pale pinkish brown to white with an indistinct pattern. *Characteristics:* Good working and gluing properties. *Uses:* Plywood core stock, hidden furniture parts, bathroom and kitchen cabinetry and some medium-priced furniture where it is finished as maple, birch or cherry under mild orange-brown maple or brown mahogany stains.

WOOD SAMPLES are handy references for identifying wood; can be obtained from mail order houses.

Ash, White *(Fraxinus americana). Source:* Eastern half of the United States except Florida, the Gulf coast and Atlantic coastal plains. *Color and Pattern:* Greyish through creamy to a reddish tinted dark brown with distinct straight grain and open pores. Quartersawn surfaces show small wood rays. *Characteristics:* Tough, supple, shock resistant, heavy, easy to work. *Uses:* Baseball bats, tool and implement handles and, because of its good bending characteristics, barrel and bent wood furniture manufacture.

Basswood *(Tilia americana)* also linden, American whitewood. *Source:* Northern U.S.A. and Canada. *Color and Pattern:* Creamy white to creamy brown, sometime reddish tinged. Small pores, faint growth rings, and wood rays darker than background on quartersawn surfaces. *Uses:* Boxes, builder's millwork and furniture where it is used for its ability to take on stains and masquerade as other woods. Often used for furniture legs. Use any color suitable to the wood being imitated which is often grained by use of glazes (See page 50).

Beech, American *(Fagus granifolia). Source:* Lake States and the Appalachian region. *Color and Pattern:* White with reddish to reddish brown tinge, pores tiny and virtually invisible. Wood rays are conspicuous on all surfaces. *Characteristics:* Heavy, shock resistant, readily steam bends, tasteless and odorless. Sometimes confused with maple, but it is lighter in weight and not as hard as maple. *Uses:* Boxes, baskets, woodenware, food containers, furniture, especially chairs and table legs. Use any of the several shades of maple, mahogany or walnut stains.

Birch, Yellow *(Betula alleghaniensis). Source:* Canada, the Lake States and New England to North Carolina. *Color and Pattern:* Creamy to light reddish brown, pores extremely small and invisible on all surfaces, wood rays visible on end grain and quartersawn surfaces, some have curly figures. *Characteristics:* Heavy, hard, strong, stiff, high shock resistance; hard working for hand tools, but machines well and takes high polish. *Uses:* Wood alcohol distillation, spools, bobbins, dowels, woodenware, furniture. Highly prized by cabinetmakers, and the best wood for imitating cherry. Use the browner versions of maple and mahogany stains.

Cherry, Black *(Prunus serotina). Source:* Maine west to the Dakotas and south along the Appalachians. *Color and Pattern:* Light to dark reddish brown,

individual pores tiny, but groupings visible in distinctive patterns, rays form flake pattern on quartersawn surfaces. *Characteristics:* Moderately heavy and hard, stiff, strong, shock resistant and hard to work with hand tools. *Uses:* Woodenware, caskets, pattern making, interior trim and furniture. Use the browner maple and mahogany stains.

Chestnut *(Castanea dentata). Source:* Eastern United States, now rare because of blight in 1900's. *Color and Pattern:* Reddish brown, open pores, coarse texture, straight grained, similar in pattern to oak, but darker. *Characteristics:* Durable, burnished surface has low to medium luster, easy to work, less splintery and more even grained than oak. *Uses:* Furniture, frames, plywood cores. Seldom found now except as wormy chestnut—the result of borers in the blighted wood. Victorian cabinetmakers used it to imitate both oak and walnut. Use walnut or oak stains, or light tan to brown pigmented distressed finishes.

Cucumber, Magnolia *(Magnolia macrophylla). Source:* Eastern States, Louisiana, and temperate Europe. *Color and Pattern:* Yellow sapwood and pale greenish-brown heartwood and indistinct pattern. Often mistaken for and sold as yellow poplar, and vice versa. *Characteristics:* Light, weak, fair workability, stringy, split-free and stains well. *Uses:* Woodenware, luggage frames and furniture panels where it is disguised as other woods. Stain to match wood being imitated.

Elm, American *(Ulmus americana). Source:* U.S.A. east of Rockies. *Color and Pattern:* Light to dark brown, sometimes reddish. End grain pores wavy with sharp light and dark boundaries, rays on quartersawn faces. *Characteristics:* Moderately heavy, hard, weak, and stiff, but has good shock resistance, good bending and excellent gluing qualities. *Uses:* Veneers, cooperage and fine furniture and bent wood chair parts. Often has Mediterranean or provincial distressed finishes, brown mahogany or walnut.

Fir including Douglas-fir and the several so-called white firs. *Source:* Pacific and Rocky Mountain States. *Color and Pattern:* White through yellowish to red with prominent textural differences in the grain with color differences in some varieties. The darker Douglas-fir has prominent and plentiful resin canals—the lighter white firs have none. *Characteristics:* Difficult to finish since resin and wild grain need to be carefully shielded by shellac or commercial wild grain and resin tamers before any type of finishing. *Uses:* Construction, millwork, cabinets, hidden parts of furniture, although some interesting use is made of wild grain in a few architectural furniture pieces.

Gum *(Liquidambar styraciflua)* also red gum, sweetgum. *Source:* Eastern and Plains States south to Texas and Florida. *Color and Pattern:* Reddish brown with occasional dark streaks, tiny pores, inconspicuous growth rings, rays on quartersawn faces. Occasionally finely figured. *Characteristics:* Hard, moderately heavy, stiff and shock resistant and requires pre-treatment for gluing. *Uses:* Veneer, plywood, interior trim, millwork and furniture. Works and carves well. Since it stains well, it was and is used to simulate other woods in furniture. Finish as red or brown mahogany or walnut.

Hickory *(Carya). Source:* Most of eastern U.S.A. except extreme northern rim and southern Florida. *Color and Pattern:* Brown to reddish brown with visible but not sharply outlined pores (as in oak and ash). Rays visible on quartersawn faces. Pores often plugged with frothy appearing material (Tyloses). *Characteristics:* Very heavy and hard, strong, stiff, and extremely shock resistant—probably toughest commercial wood. *Uses:* Tool handles, laminated skis and lawn furniture. Often shows up as parts in older oak chairs. Usually finished as oak in the graybrowns and ambers.

Mahogany, Cuban *(Swietenia mahogani)* also Puerto Rico mahogany, West Indian mahogany, etc. *Source:* The islands of the West Indies, especially Cuba. *Color and Pattern:* Yellowish tan through golden brown to brown-red with fine clear color. Available as highly figured crotch, fiddleback, mottled or plain striped. *Characteristics:* Hardest and heaviest of the true mahoganies, durable, high strength, good bending, turns and works exceptionally well, surfaces to a silky smoothness and high luster. *Uses:* Fine furniture, cabinetry and carving—becoming very rare. Finish natural, red or the more modern brown mahogany or light walnut colors.

Mahogany Honduras *(Swietenia macrophylla)* also Amazon, tropical American mahoganies. *Source:* Central America, Brazil, Mexico, Peru. *Color and Pattern:* Yellowish-brown through reddish-brown to dark, rich red with generally straighter grain than Cuban mahogany, but many figures. *Characteristics:* Extremely stable, moderately hard, heavy wood but softer and lighter in color than Cuban mahogany. *Uses:* Veneer, paneling, pattern making, ship building, and fine furniture. Same finishes as Cuban mahogany.

Mahogany, African *(Khaya ivorensis). Source:* Equatorial Africa. *Color and Pattern:* Pink to reddish or tan-brown with distinct grain; many fancy figures such as crotch, faux swirl, fiddleback, mottle, broken and plain stripe. *Characteristics:* Hard, even-textured, larger pores than mahoganies of the Americas, works and carves well, durable and strong. *Uses:* Shipbuilding, carving, cabinetry and furniture. Same finishes as Cuban mahogany.

Mahogany, Philippine—not mahogany. See Philippine Hard Woods.

Maple, Hard *(Acer saccharum)* also bird's eye, northern, rock, sugar maple. *Source:* Lake and North East States with some south to the northern rim of the southern states and eastern Texas. *Color and Pattern:* Cream to light reddish brown with very occasional green-black streaks. Pores invisible, rays prominent on quartersawn faces and visible on end and plain sawn faces as small dark flecks parallel to grain. Fancy bird's eye, curly, fiddleback, and blister figures available. *Characteristics:* Heavy, extremely hard, strong, stiff, dense, machine works and turns well, although hard with hand tools. Needs pre-drilled holes for nails and screws. *Uses:* Flooring, woodenware and furniture. Cold or red-toned maple may need tone coat of orange shellac or colored lacquer for added tone.

Oak, American White Oak *(Quercus alba),* Red Oak *(Quercus borealis). Source:* The entire eastern U.S.A. *Color and Pattern:* Light greyish-yellow-brown to light reddish brown with striking light reflecting rays of large size, and large pores. The pores of White Oak are tyloses-filled making it especially useful for watertight applications. *Characteristics:* Heavy, hard, strong, stiff, durable, with prominent open grain that requires considerable fill for a smooth surface. *Uses:* Interior trim, shipbuilding, store fixtures, watertight cooperage (white oak), and furniture. Has been finished from natural through amber to dark walnut. For darker finishes, soak with ammonia to darken wood before staining, since few stains penetrate enough to darken.

Philippine hardwoods are often misnamed mahoganies and include: Red Lauan *(Shorea negrosensis),* Tanguile *(Shorea polysperma),* Tianong *(Shorea app),* Almon *(Shorea almon),* White Lauan *(Pentacme contorta),* Bagitkan *(Parashorea picata),* Mayapis *(Shorea squamata). Source:* Philippines. *Color* and Pattern: Straw tan to dark reddish brown and, among the species, available in ribbon stripes, cross grains, and interlocking grains. Characteristics: Coarse-grained and stringy when compared to true mahoganies, although can be made to resemble them by sanding, filling and staining. They are not as stable as mahoganies. Uses: Shipbuilding, paneling, cabinet work and moderate to low-priced and unfinished furniture. Stain as mahogany or walnut.

Pine, White, means different things with different periods: eastern white pine (punkin pine) for Early American pieces, and western white pine (pinus monticola) in most modern pine pieces. They are very similar. Western pine is a little harder. Color and Pattern: Cream to light reddish brown with visible resin canals and gradual color changes across subdued growth rings. Characteristics: Soft, moderately light, stiff and shock resistant; works, glues and nails well. Uses: Construction, millwork, veneer, siding and furniture, usually reproductions or unfinished. Use brown maple or mahogany—or use fabric dyes, wiping stain or enamels.

Poplar, Yellow (Liriodendron tulipifera), Whitewood, Tulipwood and sometimes cucumber. Source: New England to Michigan and the Appalachians. Color and Pattern: Canary to brownish-yellow with a greenish tinge, barely visible pores, even textured and straight-grained. Characteristics: Medium to light weight, moderately soft, stiff and shock resistant; works well, holds paint, enamel, stain and glue well and is odorless and tasteless. Uses: Veneer, pulpwood and furniture where its staining characteristics make it excellent for simulating other woods. Color to match wood being imitated.

Redwood (Sequoia sempervirens). Source: California fog belt north of San Francisco to Oregon. Color and Pattern: Deep reddish-brown with alternating glossy and matte ring textures. Characteristics: Light, moderately hard, stiff, strong, only fair shock resistance. Seasoned wood stable, works and finishes well. Resists decay and termites. Appearance similar to Western red cedar but has no odor or taste, unlike the pungent cedar. Uses: Construction, millwork, tanks and outdoor furniture. Natural, or silvery grays, browns, and blacks work well.

Rosewood, Brazilian (Dalbergia nigra) also jacaranda. Source: Brazil. Color and Pattern: Mixed browns, dark browns, chocolate and purple violet with conspicuous black streaks. Characteristics:

Larger pores than the East Indian varieties. Heavy, very hard, stiff, hard to work with hand tools. Uses: Musical instruments, fine furniture, especially Danish imports. Wipe with lacquer thinner and finish natural.

Rosewood, East Indian (Dahlbergia latifolia), Bombay rosewood, Malobar. Source: Ceylon and South India. Color and Pattern: Pinkish brown to purplish with dark and light streaks. Characteristics: Very hard, very heavy, coarse-textured, fair ease of working, burnishes to a dull gloss. Uses: Veneer, musical instruments, cabinetry and fine furniture, often seen in Chinese imports. Finish natural.

Teak (Tectona grandis). Source: Burma, East India, Indo-China, Java. Color and Pattern: Yellow, tan through dark brown with light and dark streaks, and patterned surprisingly like walnut. Characteristics: Heavy, strong, oily and tough. Uses: Veneer, shipbuilding, floor parquet, paneling and fine furniture, usually Oriental or Scandinavian. Finish natural or darken with brown stains.

Walnut, American (Juglans nigra), black walnut. Source: Vermont to Nebraska and south to Georgia and Texas. Color and Pattern: Light brown to a purple-chocolate brown with pores visible as dark grooves and streaks; variety of figures only matched by mahogany. Characteristics: Heavy, strong, stable, stiff, good shock resistance; machines and works well. Uses: Veneer, gunstocks, paneling, novelties, carving, and furniture where it is most popular of North American hardwoods. Becoming rare as veneer and lumber. Finish natural or darken with brown or black-brown stain.

Walnut, Claro (Juglans, hindsii), California walnut; said to be a descendant of Juglans regia, the European walnut. Source: Coastal strip of California and southern Oregon. Color and Pattern: Tan-brown and dark brown with prominent light stripes and a wavy grain. Available in crotch, fiddleback and swirl figures. Characteristics: Softer and more open-grained than American walnut. Very rare. Finish same as American walnut.

Walnut, Circassian (Juglans regia), English, French, Italian, Persian or European Walnut. Source: Europe. Color and Pattern: Tawny-colored with streaks of dark brown or black. Characteristics: Weaker but otherwise similar to American walnut. Uses: Veneer, paneling, gun stocks, and fine furniture, usually English or European. Finish same as American walnut.

Preparing the Wood Surface

HARD SPRAY from garden hose will quickly help to remove finish already loosened by wash-off removers.

Have you ever watched a person walk up to a fine piece of furniture, run his finger tips over the finish, then drop his palm to stroke the surface? Besides the distinctive, warm, velvet touch of a good finish on fine wood, he may be feeling for waves, nibs and other slight imperfections in the finish.

A glass-smooth surface ordinarily indicates that it was probably made or resurfaced after the advent of machine planing and sanding. Slight waves parallel to the grain indicate that it was probably hand levelled prior to 1850 with a plane having a very slightly bowed cutting edge on the plane iron.

Detecting Defects

Any other defects detected by the finger tips and palm can indicate the craftsman's carelessness in preparing the surface and applying the finish. Slight valleys or dents, with no apparent surface damage, indicate poor level sanding or a failure to raise local dents, dings or pressure marks by water or steam swelling. Almost invisible, but readily detected by hand, small truncated cones indicate dust or fiber nibs that were not eliminated by sufficient level sanding and rubbing.

Invariably the same person will look for signs of a muddy finish caused by erect wood fibers in the clear surface coating or for fragments of filler or pigment in the top surface coating. A good craftsman stiffens the wood fibers with shellac or glue size so that the fibers can be sanded off. He also shields the filler or pigments from the top surface coats with an application of protective wash coats.

For a pleasing finish, remove all the flaws from your finishing projects by conscientiously preparing the surface first.

Preparing the Surface

Fine wood finishes should never be attempted over damaged finish, or, over a dirty, rough, or damaged surface. The first task is to clean, repair and smooth the surface (after removing all handles, pulls and detachable pieces, like vanity table mirrors). On raw wood (unfinished furniture), smooth by sanding (covered in next chapter) and repair any flaws exposed by the smoothing.

On furniture with an old finish, remove as much of the finish with a paint and varnish remover as necessary to reach a good foundation for the new finish. Usually all of the old finish should be removed.

Commercial paint and varnish removers range from simple liquid solvent mixtures through thick, syrup-like combinations with evaporation retarding agents (often waxes and wax derivatives), to paste-thick preparations that will cling to vertical surfaces. Some removers are designed for solvent cleanup, some for water or detergent and water cleanup, and some for "no cleanup." Both flammable and non-flammable removers are available.

Your choice of remover depends largely on your own preferences, practices, place of use, material to be stripped and, eventually, experience. It is wasteful to use a thick paste-type remover on a small shellacked box when denatured alcohol or a 50/50 denatured alcohol-lacquer thinner mixture will do the job faster and with little or no cleanup problems. On the other hand, if you are working anywhere near an open flame, pilot light, or a circuit that might cause open sparks, use one of the safer, non-flammable removers.

On large furniture projects, the paste-type remover is best, especially if the furniture cannot be turned to place the working surface in a horizontal position. If regluing of the furniture is necessary, complete the gluing prior to the stripping of the old finish.

Apply ample remover to one surface at a time, covering only a small area that can be easily stripped before the remover dries out. Flow the remover on the surface, with minimum brushing.

On stubborn finishes, cover the applied remover with a sheet of aluminum foil or wax paper to retard evaporation so that a single coat will often soften the finish where two or more coats would otherwise be necessary.

The remover action is completed when the old finish appears wrinkled and lifted and is softened through to the wood. To determine the effectiveness of the remover, place your finger tip on a test area. If it moves down to the wood (or to a different layer in the case of a multi-layered paint coating) the remover has done its task.

Then take a flexible putty knife with rounded

LYE—TRICKY BUT USEFUL

Lye can discolor, chemically "burn," and soften wood. It also can remove multiple, age-hardened layers of paint faster than any other method. To obtain this benefit and minimize the chance of lye's damaging effects, use it only on old multiple-paint coatings, and stop its action before it has a chance to get to the wood.

Work out-of-doors on a warm day, and have a garden hose handy.

Make a strong lye solution by dissolving a can of lye for each quart of water. Never have the container more than half full, and *never* use an aluminum or plastic container. The lye causes the water to heat short of boiling; the plastic might rupture, and aluminum is attacked by lye. Cornstarch or wallpaper paste (about ¼ cup per quart of solution) can be added to thicken the mix for use on vertical surfaces.

Before you proceed, have ready a bucket of water and a large bottle of vinegar for neutralizing the lye.

Use a wooden-handled cotton dish mop to apply the lye mix. The warmer the day, the faster the lye will work, so check every minute or two with a knife blade to see if the paint layers are coming loose.

When it appears that the lye is starting to work on the last layer, stop its action. Hose the surface thoroughly to remove all traces of lye. Then scrub all surfaces with full-strength vinegar to neutralize the lye. Scrape off all remaining loose paint. Allow the surface to dry for several hours. Apply a solvent-type remover to completely strip any remaining finish.

Don't use lye near vegetation for it will ruin the area.

Any lye that gets on you or your clothes must be washed off with large amounts of water, then flushed with vinegar to neutralize it. Lye isn't instantaneously painful, but if left on the skin for more than a few seconds it can be painful. Lye in an eye can cause blindness.

Lye can attack wood fibers if left on too long; be especially sure to wash lye out of joints, corners, and cracks. Discoloration from lye can range from mild to severe but it can be bleached out with one or more applications of oxalic acid.

Obviously, lye is not recommended as a general purpose remover. Save this "big gun" remover for those occasional tough battles with oak chairs or pine tables having numerous coats of paint.

Use Trisodium phosphate (commonly sold as T.S.P.) as a remover similar in action to lye. Dissolve a pound of T.S.P. in a gallon of hot water and use it exactly as you would lye. It is slower and less corrosive than lye but will still discolor many woods.

COVER REMOVER with foil to prevent evaporation. Finish will stick to foil making pickup easier.

UNCOVERED REMOVER will dry quickly; may not penetrate to original surface. Scraping is required.

WRINKLED SURFACE appears when remover is applied to paints, enamels, varnishes; remove by scraping or with a strong jet from a garden hose.

USE SWABS and picks to remove loosened old finish in small areas such as carvings, molding, corners. Any remover left on surface will damage finish.

edges and corners to prevent gouging and scratching and gently slide the finish-remover mass off the surface. Work with a clean knife, and wipe it frequently, so you can see what you are doing. Quarter or half sheets of newspaper work well as knife wipes.

Drop all wipes and waste remover into a can for immediate disposal. The waste will mar any finish it touches, and the fumes are a health and fire hazard. Remember, too enthusiastic use of the putty knife can gouge, scratch or slice the wood surface that has been temporarily softened by remover. Be firm but gentle, and do not attempt to scrape the surface.

Remove all traces of the remover from the surface by following the manufacturer's recommendations. Many professionals insist on denatured alcohol (shellac thinner grade) as the only, or, at least the final cleaner. It appears to pick up waxes and carry them off without spreading them. Work it gently across the surface with clean No. 2/0 steel wool pads, then wipe with a clean cloth or paper towel.

Use Caution

Do *not* use wood or methyl alcohol, antifreeze or other non-shellac grade alcohols. Wood or methyl alcohol fumes can be extremely harmful. Less expensive non-shellac-solvent grade denatured alcohols, such as antifreeze grades, often contain non-drying petroleum or coal tar distillates as denaturants.

Use steel wool, brushes, sticks, knife blades—anything that works—to remove all traces of remover from cracks, joints, corners, carvings, etc.

Allow the piece to dry completely. Examine all stripped surfaces for skips, spots or streaks that need removing. Reapply remover with padded sticks to small areas, and repeat the cleanup process locally.

Repairs May be Necessary

Look for defects that need repairing—gouges, cracks, dents, loose veneer, loose joints; broken, missing or loose spindles, splats, stretchers, etc.

A minimum kit of tools for repairing consists of a 4-way or shoe rasp, a sturdy knife, steel wool, abrasive papers and a putty knife. Additional tools for greater ease of working or for special jobs would include: a half-round file, flat, round and half-round Surform rasps, linoleum knife, spatula, palette knife, drill and bits, chisels, glue injector, C-clamps, wood clamps, bar clamps and web clamps. Most of the tools in the second list can be

TOOLS for finishing, refinishing, and woodworking. 1. Pipe clamp. 2. Bar clamp. 3. Chisels. 4. Rasps. 5. File. 6. Linoleum knife. 7. Spatula. 8. Drill and bits. 9. C-clamp. 10. Belt clamp. 11. Saw. 12. Sandpaper. 13. Glue syringe. 14. 4-way rasp. 15. Putty knife. 16. Knife. 17. Steel wool.

FIRST STEP of disassembling furniture joints is to remove all screws, bolts, or other fasteners.

USE SOFT-FACED MALLET to disassemble glueless dowel joints (a hammer will dent the surface).

replaced with a little ingenuity—a flexible knife blade for a spatula, string or ropes for clamps, abrasive paper around shaped sticks for half-round rasps, etc.

Double check the places that need repairing and repair them in a logical order. Normally it is best to repair loose joints first—preferably by disassembly, cleaning and regluing. However, if a gouge or veneer blister would be easier to reach and repair with the joint loose or disassembled, repair that first.

Repair joints by complete disassembly, removal of old glues, with minimum damage to wood. Reglue with wood or cloth shims if necessary. Hot water applied locally with small pads of cloth or paper towel softens old hot glues. You will need a knife, chisel or scraper to remove most modern glues.

Where joints cannot satisfactorily be disassembled, glue may be injected by a hypodermic-like glue injector (available at craft supply stores) or by alternately rocking the joint and forcing the glue into the joint. In some cases, one of the so-called "wood-swelling" materials available at hardware counters may do the job, especially if you add a locking dowel.

Remember, neither glue nor wood-sweller can do the job if the joint isn't a good press-fit to start with. It may be necessary to shape and glue extra wood to one or more parts of the joint. It may be best to fill-in and recut the mortise or socket, especially on dowel joints. In rectangular mortise-and-tenon joints, shimming works well.

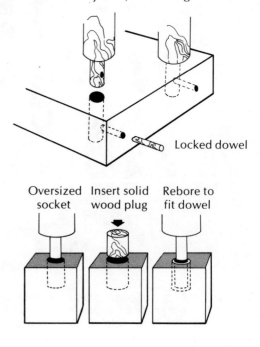

Locked dowel

Oversized socket   Insert solid wood plug   Rebore to fit dowel

REMOVE OLD GLUE from disassembled joints with cloth or paper pads dipped in warm water.

INJECT GLUE near end of joint through a previously drilled 3/32-inch hole with plastic glue syringe.

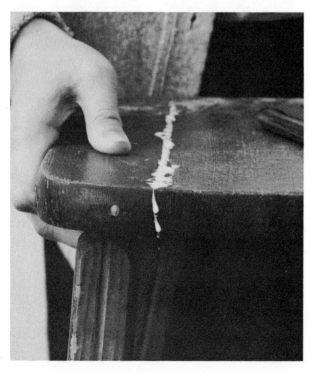

ROCK CRACK OPEN until glue placed on surface works well into the length and breadth of the break.

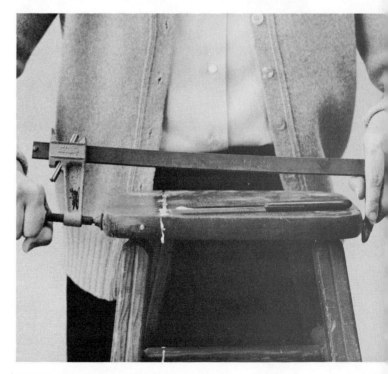

USE CLAMP to keep the newly glued joint securely in place until the glue is thoroughly dry.

Patching of large gouges, broken edges, missing veneers or deep burns can often be accomplished by inlaying a piece of matching wood or using a synthetic patching material. Inlay patching works best when you choose a piece of wood that very nearly matches the damaged piece and is cut to follow the grain pattern—not merely a regular rectangle or circle. Before cutting the patch, place the damaged piece between you and a light source and rotate the patch piece to determine if the lay of wood fibers in the patch matches both the grain and reflection characteristics of the original. Grain can be blended but not reflection differences.

Before inlaying patch or veneer, remove all old glue by scraping or, in the case of older hot glues, soaking it off with hot water and a small pad of paper toweling. Clamp the patch block or veneer in place with firm but gentle pressure. Use aluminum foil or plastic wrap and a wood backup block between the surface and clamp.

Use the smallest amount of glue that will do the job (preferably plastic resin woodworkers glue available at hardware stores). Glue cleanup takes time, can damage the new repair and interferes with the staining and finishing processes.

Try to remove glue before it hardens by slicing it off with a very sharp knife or chisel, then wiping with a warm, moist rag. Synthetic patching materials are available in tubes, cans and sticks as prepared putties and with lacquers, vinyl, oil or water-mix bases. All are applied to thoroughly clean concave surfaces, preferably rough or undercut, and built up according to the manufacturer's instructions to a slightly convex top surface which will allow for drying shrinkage and can be sanded level.

Blend patches into surrounding area with locally applied stain. With less absorbent synthetics, it may be necessary to use a pigmented wiping stain (see page 29).

Replacement of missing parts should be done with the age and condition of the original in mind. A well-worn, 100-year-old kitchen chair does not look good with a bright, new birch dowel stretcher. Try to find a suitable piece of old matching wood.

Second hand stores, thrift shops, junk stores and junk yards are good places to look for table leaves from mahogany, cherry, walnut, oak and other "furniture wood" tables. Old, weathered axe and

PLACE VENEER PATCH over damaged area; use knife to outline its shape cutting to a 1/16-inch depth.

USE SMALL CHISEL or knife to remove damaged area; follow wood grain to avoid any splitting, chipping.

GLUE PATCH in place; avoid using too much glue as excess around the edges is hard to remove.

HOLD PATCH in place with heavy flat object; use foil or wax paper as shield between weight and patch.

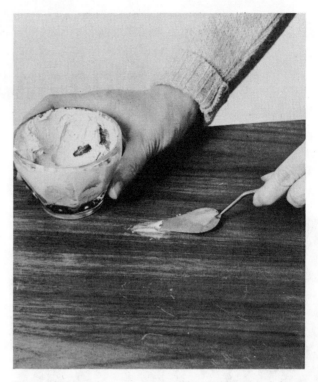

ALTERNATE METHOD of patching is to chisel out damaged area so that recess has overhanging edges.

FILL RECESS with putty-type patching compound; form slightly convex surface to allow for shrinkage.

sledge hammer handles supply hickory. Ash can be found in garden tool handles. Birch is used in broom handles. Collecting furniture "wrecks" keeps many a furniture restorer in fine aged wood. Old rural buildings are veritable treasure troves of aged wood—if you get there first!

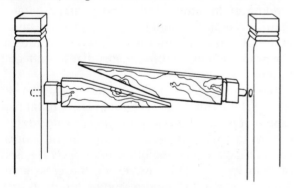

Replacement of spindles, splats, stretchers or any parts of furniture that are mortised into other parts at both ends can be a problem if disassembly of the furniture is impossible. Make the replacement part a fraction of an inch too long, then make a diagonal cut through the piece with a thin saw blade where the grain or decoration would tend to hide the cut or scarf joint. If the piece is thick enough, a spline insert will increase the strength.

WHAT TO DO ABOUT WARP

Most wood becomes warped because the convex surface has more moisture in the wood fibers than the concave side. If the board is finished or moisture-protected on one side only, that side will be concave and the other, or unprotected side, will be convex. Dry the convex side or add moisture to the concave side, or both, then allow several days for moisture content to even out. When the surfaces are thoroughly dry, finish **BOTH** sides and all edges.

It may be necessary to cut the board parallel to the centerline of the warp curve into several 4-inch widths. Turn alternate 4-inch cuttings over, and edge-glue the reassembled board for surfacing.

The least destructive method is to saw-kerf the convex side to within 1/8 inch of cutting through to the concave surface. Space the kerfs across the convex surface to provide even distribution. Experiment so that just enough kerfs are made so the board can be gently straightened out. When the required kerfs have been cut, apply glue, and, if necessary, long thin shims can be added to permit perfect flattening of the board. When the glue dries, glue one or more cleats across the board at right angles to the glued kerfs.

Smoothing and Coloring Wood

SANDING *either by hand or by machine is a basic step in all finishing and refinishing projects.*

Many finishing defects can be forestalled at the smoothing stage. Hours can be spent following staining, finishing and rubbing procedures, but the results can be disappointing. A muddy, pitted finish with a hazy grain pattern reveals upon close examination that poor smoothing is the major cause. For example, sanding at right angles to the grain makes the grain or figure pattern hazy by presenting an overlay of competing texture. Wood fibers that should have been removed in final sanding may remain standing straight up through the finish layers to give a muddy, spotty finish. An improperly filled and sealed open-grained wood has a muddy, cratered look where voids are left and filler has been lifted into the finish coats.

For fine furniture, perform all finish sanding *with the grain.* Only by sanding with the grain can you hope to get maximum smoothing with minimum waste of wood and effort.

Power Sanders

Disk and drum sanders are not advised for the fine sanding of furniture. Both sanders are extremely hard to handle accurately and remove too much material too fast. The disk sander, in addition, leaves cross-grain sanding marks that are difficult to remove.

The sander that is probably sold most often to the amateur craftsman is the standard orbital pad sander. It is advertised as providing the most sander for the lowest price. It will do a lot of general carpentry grade sanding but should never be used on thin veneers. On thin veneer, the cross grain scratches produced require sanding too deep, and cutting through the veneer before achieving a smooth, blemish-free surface is a risk.

One or two very high speed, 10,000–12,000 orbits per-minute, small orbit (⅛ inch or less) sanders now on the market can be used for all but the final two or three grades in finish sanding. But beware—because of their high speed, they cut faster than you might expect!

On the other hand, a straight line sander, used with the grain, makes cuts that follow the grain and are therefore easier to smooth out.

Best of the straight line sanders is the belt sander, which, after some practice, will handle anything from the rough through the final sanding to fine polishing (with the recently available nylon polishing belts).

Next are the "in-line" pad sanders, which are often available as mechanically switched orbital/in-line combinations driven by drill-type universal motors. These combinations are extremely useful and cost only a little more than either member alone. They are usually less costly than most belt sanders and only use halves, thirds or quarters of a standard 9 × 11-inch sheet of abrasive paper. They will usually handle as heavy a job as you will have—particularly the combination in-line/orbital variety, although it is slower than the belt sander.

A good device for final smoothing and rubbing is the heavy duty vibrating or "buzzer"-type pad sander. It is built like an old-fashioned magnetic door buzzer and gives very fast, short, in-line strokes which give beautiful final smoothing and rubbing results, but it is extremely slow for heavier work where much surface leveling is required.

IN-LINE SANDERS should be used for finishing projects where perfectly smooth surface is desired.

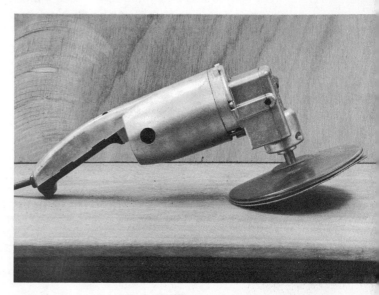

DISK SANDERS are hard to control; can often create deep swirl marks which are difficult to remove.

ORBITAL SANDERS are good for first sanding, should not be used for smoothing before applying finish.

BELT SANDERS provide the fastest in-line sanding but require practice in handling for fine finishing.

Sanding by Hand

As handy as electrically-driven sanders are, you will discover that some means for holding abrasive paper for hand sanding is needed. Automatic, self-feeding and simple metal, plastic or rubber block varieties are available at most hardware and craft stores. Somehow, situations always arise where commercial sanding blocks just won't fit. Follow the general instructions below for hints on making your own sanding blocks.

Back abrasive papers with a resilient rubber, felt, cork, or carpet. It is a temptation to place a piece of garnet paper against a flat plywood block and start sanding on the theory that you want a flat surface, and the block is flat. This is not so. Any grit or dust getting between the block and paper produces a high spot that heats up and gouges its way across the surface that you are trying to smooth. Also, any dust clogs between the abrasive grains on the cutting side can pick up loose grit and gouge the surface. With a resilient backup,

these otherwise unavoidable mishaps are greatly minimized, if not completely avoided.

The size of the sanding block you use for a given job will depend largely on your own preferences. However, keep in mind that it is a lot easier to obtain a truly flat surface by using a large block area than by using a small one. It is also a lot easier to cut through and ruin the surface with a small one. A good policy is to use as large a block as is comfortable for a given job; and the smaller the block the greater care you should take to prevent cutting through the surface. An eighth of a standard abrasive paper sheet is a good minimum size.

Unless you intend to do a lot of rough sanding of old, multi-layered paint or varnish surfaces don't bother with sand or flint papers. They are dull, slow-cutting, clogging, and grit-dropping. In spite of their low initial cost, they will cost you much more in time, temper, and money than garnet or aluminum oxide papers.

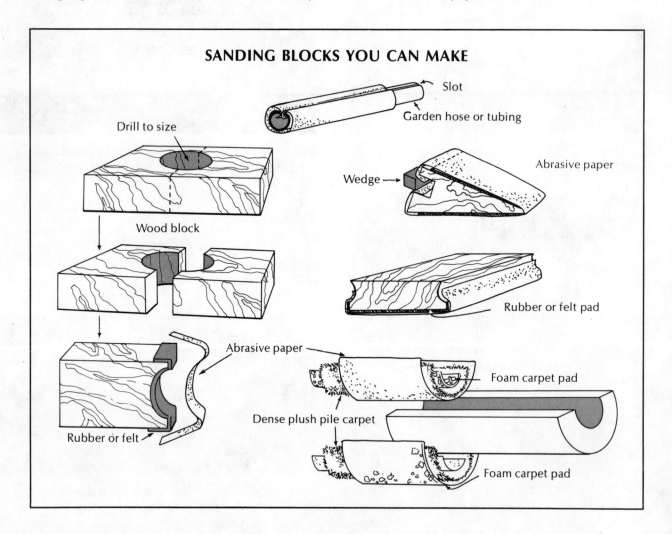

SANDING BLOCKS YOU CAN MAKE

Slot

Garden hose or tubing

Drill to size

Wood block

Wedge

Abrasive paper

Rubber or felt pad

Abrasive paper

Rubber or felt

Foam carpet pad

Dense plush pile carpet

Foam carpet pad

Garnet paper is a reddish abrasive paper that has a good "tooth" to it and has the happy characteristics of being just hard enough to cut well and yet fracture enough to keep presenting new cutting edges.

Aluminum oxide paper is a gray-black, tough, hard abrasive and is stocked by the better hardware and craft stores. It is one of the most versatile papers for the wood finisher. Especially useful are the "open coat" aluminum oxide papers that cut down drastically on paper clogging.

Silicon carbide paper is a black, hard abrasive that is used in the metal finishing trades and for wood finishing with finer grits and specialty or non-loading papers.

A Smoothing Formula

Examine the piece to be smoothed in a good light directed at a shallow angle off the surface. Locate all major defects, mark them with chalk or pencil rubbings and mentally match them to the finest grit that will practically level out the defects. A test board showing the surface effect of the several major grits is handy.

Starting with the finest grit that will do the job, proceed down through the grits to achieve the desired surface. Remember, as soon as the surface is level and homogeneously abraded, with no cuts or scratches deeper than those produced by the grit, it is time to go to the next finer grit.

Between sandings, brush and wipe the surface off thoroughly. A stray lump of 80-grit getting under the 280 or 320-grit sanding block can groove its way across a smooth cherry table top.

When using the medium fine to fine grits, or on any grade where increased flexibility of the backing is desired, dampen the backing (smooth side) with a sponge or rag moistened, but not wet, with lukewarm water. The greater flexibility acquired allows closer surface contact, faster and cleaner cutting, and less clogging or glazing of the grit. Shiny, glazed, or loaded spots MUST be knocked out, brushed off, or cleaned off with thinner and alcohol and thoroughly dried before re-use. Loaded or glazed spots will pick up grit and scratch smooth surfaces.

For fine polished finishes, many professionals use worn abrasive papers long after most of us throw them away. Their advantages are these: Prior use has virtually eliminated any oversize grains or clumps that too often cause initial problems with new paper. Worn papers also produce an extremely

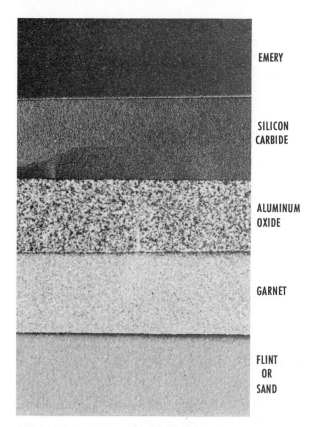

EMERY

SILICON CARBIDE

ALUMINUM OXIDE

GARNET

FLINT OR SAND

ABRASIVE PAPERS are available in various "grits" (see page 33). Aluminum oxide is most widely used.

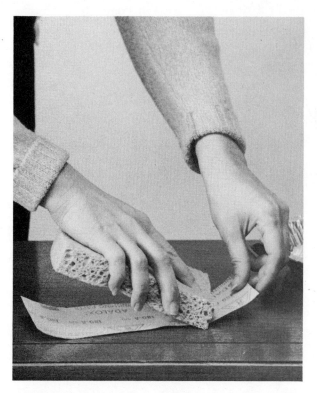

MOISTEN BACKS of finer grits to increase their flexibility (do not let water touch the grit face).

homogeneously ground surface. Their main disadvantage is that they tend to be slower working as they get older and worn down.

Scuffing two identical papers together grit-to-grit is a way to "age" paper.

When striving for perfect surface preparation, you will reach a point where you will find that instead of further smoothing, you seem merely to be moving fuzz around. At this point, sponge the surface with just enough warm, clean water to thoroughly wet it, but not to leave a visible film. Too much water can damage thin veneers. Some professionals add a few drops of "wetting agent," obtainable at chemical and photographic suppliers, to encourage uniform wetting and penetration of the surface. Allow the surface to dry thoroughly —at least overnight—before leveling any raised grain or fibers by resanding with the same size grit as last used before sponging.

Sponging performs two valuable functions: it raises both the grain and wood fibers so that they can be leveled off, forestalling problems at later stages; it also swells out any pressure marks, dimples, or "dings" made during handling.

If any hairs or wood fibers remain, they may be sized or stiffened for removal by sanding. Brush with a dilute shellac sizing-sealer (1 part 4-pound cut shellac to 4 parts denatured alcohol brushed on as a single thin coat), a commercial sanding

SCUFF ABRASIVE PAPERS together face-to-face before use to remove any oversized or loose grit.

sealer, or a non-sealing glue size. If you intend to use water stains, glue sizing is preferable, because it allows good stain penetration. The glue sizing is a simple mixture of ¼ cup of flake hide glue to one gallon of water. Brush it lightly and evenly over the surface, leaving no heavy trailing film. Keep hands and metals off, since it may stain. Any stains that show up can usually be removed by careful use of chlorine or oxalic acid bleaches. Allow the surface to dry thoroughly, then carefully sand with the same size grit as last used. Applied and sanded correctly, glue sizing produces a beautiful, clear surface, with virtual disappearance of the glue itself.

Bleaching

Bleach is useful in finishing for removing or lightening color in local areas or entire surfaces, preparatory to application of new color or simply to enliven the surface.

For furniture use there are basically three bleaches, listed in order of increasing strength: chlorinated laundry bleach, oxalic acid, and commercial, two-solution wood bleach.

To apply bleach, use only synthetic fiber brushes (nylon), because natural fibers are attacked by all bleaches. Use plastic or rubber gloves and wear old clothes.

Chlorinated liquid laundry bleach provides slight to moderate lightening of some natural wood colors. Successive applications remove similar amounts of color, thus giving some bleaching control in mottled or stained areas. This bleach also removes some chemical, dye, ink, and water stains.

Oxalic acid, in saturated solution, makes an excellent bleach, not only for the natural wood colors but also for many water and chemical stains. It is particularly useful for removing alkali, rust, and soap stains from old oak. Oxalic acid may be used in less than saturated solutions for milder bleaching. Neutralize the acid with a cool solution of borax (1 cup borax per quart of hot water), rinse off with clear water, wipe, then dry thoroughly before further finishing.

Two-solution bleaches are extremely strong. With one or more applications they will bleach the wood as light as you need—probably lighter. Follow instructions exactly, and don't take any short cuts— they can be dangerous and costly. Ingredients and instructions differ enough so that you *MUST* read and follow directions.

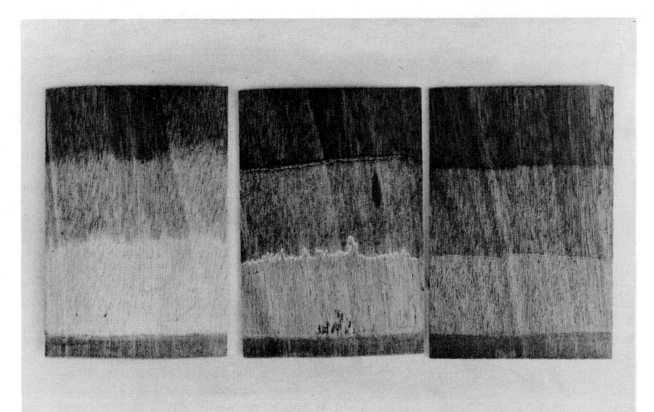

BLEACHED SAMPLES of lauan wood show a range of light to heavy bleaching. Sample at left used a 2-solution peroxide bleach, center sample used oxalic acid, and the sample on the right used household chlorine bleach. Dark strip at bottom of each was resanded to natural color.

HOW TO MAKE GLUE SIZE

Glue size can be made up from standard cabinet-maker's hide glue. If the household workshop has a hot-glue pot with cabinet-maker's hide glue, use a mix of 1 part hot glue to 45 parts hot water. If you have the dry granules of glue, ¼ cup of the granules to a gallon of hot water is a good starting point for experimenting. Unfortunately, there are enough differences in hide glues and granules to make it impossible to give an exact dry glue to water formula. If cabinet glue is hard to find locally, try an art supply store; it may carry rabbit skin glue, a more refined and expensive version.

Once you have the granules of glue, you can make the cabinet-maker's hot glue with the following recipe: One pound of granules or flakes to be covered with cold water so that there is ⅛ inch of clear water above the solids. Soak for 20 minutes — the water will be absorbed — and then heat in a double boiler to about 180° F. The granule-water mix will thicken. Correct viscosity is that point at which the glue drips off a stick in a thin, continuous stream instead of in droplets. You will probably have to add a little hot water to reach this flow point.

CHECK TEMPERATURE of glue to make sure it does not exceed 180° F. Stir mixture continually.

FOAMING ACTION is typical of 2-solution peroxide bleach at work on clean and smooth wood surface.

In all bleaching be sure the surface is smooth and clean, so that you can see differences in color. Be sure the surface is free of grease, finish, and wax, so that the water solution of bleach can penetrate evenly into the surface. If you have trouble getting penetration, use fine steel wool, waterproof abrasive paper, or nylon abrasive mesh to "work the surface" and promote penetration.

Remember that with any true bleach you are applying water solutions to a wood surface, and that most bleaches will soften (temporarily) and raise the grain and wood fibers. It may be necessary and wise to perform the glue sizing and sanding operation after the bleach.

Also, remember that any bleach is liable to leave some chemical residue in the wood surface that may become air-borne during subsequent sanding operations. A lightweight painter's mask for nose and mouth is a good investment.

Two types of products are available that are often erroneously called wood bleaches: the so-called lacquer or varnish lighteners, which "lighten" in the sense that they do not darken wood; and light-colored pigmented wiping stains which leave a light pigment on the surface, thus "lightening" the wood. Both are excellent in their place, but should not be called bleaches.

PEROXIDE BLEACHED TABLE TOP is bone-white in color; visual grain effects are almost completely gone.

BLEACH SAFETY

When using bleaches, it is a good idea to wear rubber gloves and old clothes. All bleaches should be washed off the skin with water as soon as possible.

Chlorinated bleaches may seem tame, since they are so familiar, but they can cause uncomfortable skin problems when used at full strength. Oxalic acid can cause burns if it is left on the skin or gets in the eyes. Whenever sanding wood known or suspected to have been treated with oxalic acid that may not have been completely neutralized, wear a painter's nose-and-mouth mask, as oxalic acid mixed in the air with sawdust can irritate the lungs and mucous membrane. Wash oxalic acid off any part of the body with large quantities of water.

The two-solution bleaches must be washed off immediately if they get on the skin. The first liquid usually is a caustic alkali, and the second often is extremely strong hydrogen peroxide. Both can cause severe problems if left on the skin for more than a few seconds.

Stains—Dyes and Pigments

There are some conditions and preferred methods that should be observed for a successful staining job:

1. The wood surface must be uniformly smooth and clean. Any roughness or variation in smoothness will probably show up as differences in penetration or surface buildup. Any masking dirt interferes with your judgment of color.

2. The surface must be free of old finish, wax, or grease to prevent interference with stain penetration or surface buildup.

3. Use synthetic bristle brushes with brass or rubber ferrules to prevent rust stains.

4. Start staining areas that are least visible and progress to more visible areas to allow adjustment of color or technique before working visible surface.

5. Try to work single surfaces at a time—back, sides, top. Try to work with the surface horizontal. Avoid edge-drip and splatter.

6. Where vertical surfaces are unavoidable, work from the bottom up with continuous edge-to-edge strokes paralleling the grain—this minimizes drips and overlap marks.

7. Work areas in such a way as to allow succeeding strokes to butt against still-wet edges. Butting against dry edges leads to dark overlap marks.

8. In most cases, start with a lighter rather than a darker stain. It is easy to add color but very difficult to lighten a stain without causing mottling on the surface.

9. Where lightening is necessary, apply the appropriate solvent. Use plenty of clean rags to wipe the solvent off immediately.

10. Work the stain into pores of open-grained wood, like oak, to prevent spotty, light-pored effect obtained if the stain bridges or "jumps over" some pores.

11. Beware of any but the lightest touch-up sanding on stained surfaces—use 600-grit or finer. Even a partial cut-through will show up light.

12. If you make a mistake, use a commercial bleach, and start over with the advantage of newly acquired experience.

Water stains are true dyes dissolved in water. They are transparent and by far the cheapest, most permanent, and most easily handled of the penetrating stains. They also have the broadest range of

APPLY STAIN to small area that is least visible and check for desired color tone and density.

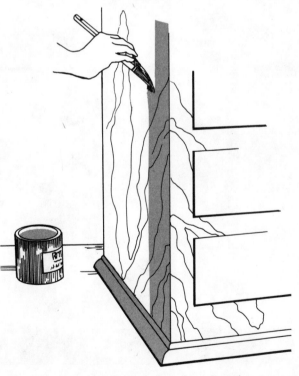

FOLLOW GRAIN of the wood working from bottom to top on all vertical surfaces; avoid edge drips.

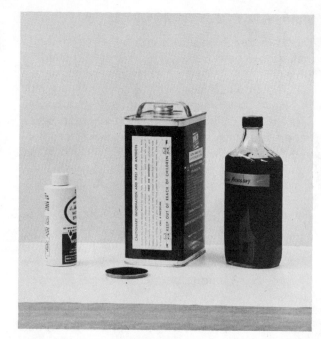

WATER STAIN POWDER at left is mixed with hot water to produce the most durable, clearest wood stains.

SPIRIT STAIN POWDERS mixed with alcohol provide a range of colors which are cool and subtle in tone.

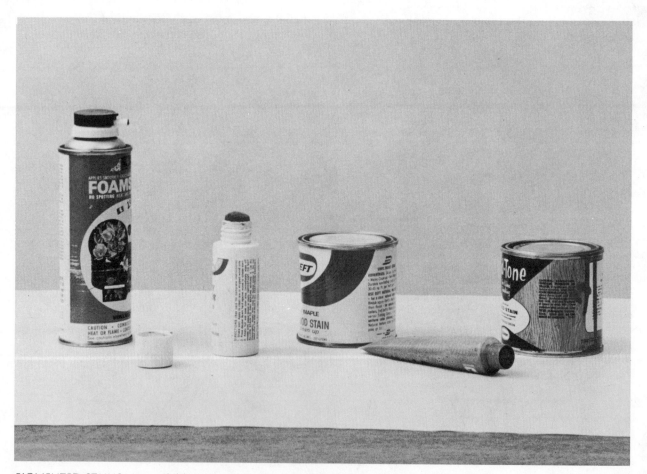

PIGMENTED STAINS are available in liquid form in foam producing aerosol cans and dauber top bottles and cans; pastes and creams come in tubes. Oil based stains come only in cans.

OAK BOARD shows effect of water, spirit, vinyl pigment, and oil pigment stain application in identical amounts. Clarity of grain is far greater for both water and spirit stains than that of pigment stain.

brilliant, warm-toned colors. Their disadvantage is that they raise the grain and require at least 24 hours drying time. A thorough pre-sponging or glue sizing and sanding to minimize grain-raising problems and ample drying time are normally small prices to pay for the many advantages of water stains.

When applying stain by brush or spray, the area covered and direction of movement should be controlled, so that each succeeding stroke runs along a wet stain edge. To run along a dried edge invites spreading into the dry stained area with resulting dark overlap marks.

Spirit (alcohol) stains are dyes dissolved in alcohol. They are slightly less permanent, extremely fast drying, and generally cooler in tone—with a greenish cast—than water dyes. Because of their speed in drying, experience is required to avoid overlap marks.

Non-grain-raising stains, usually listed as N.G.R. stains, can be either water or spirit stains with non-grain-raising solvents used. They are usually faster-drying than water stains, less difficult to use than spirit stains. But they are more expensive and not readily available in as wide a range of brilliant

colors as the water stains. Also, they tend to go wild in wide-grained soft woods, like fir and pine, with a pronounced zebra effect.

Oil stains are dyes dissolved in oils. For many years they were used widely in industry, but, because of their tendency to fade, they have been almost totally replaced by water, spirit, or N.G.R. stains.

Sealer stains are essentially sealers, diluted lacquer, shellac, or varnish with dyes dissolved in suitable thinners. They tend to exhibit the characteristics of their particular solvent category above, and provide less surface penetration than other stains.

Pigmented wiping stains should really be called paint products, not stains, because they are ground pigments suspended in a vehicle—although some dyes may be present. The identification tipoff on these is the instruction to mix or stir well before using. They are used where you desire either to accentuate the grain pattern by color fill-in of the open pores, or to mask the grain pattern to obtain an overall color. Wiping stains may be used to fake another wood. Since they tend to be surface "paints," they are relatively easy to use, patch up, and rework. However, it is not advisable to mask a fine cabinet wood with these paint products except for very special effects.

Almost every imaginable vehicle has been used for pigmented wiping stains: shellac, lacquers, varnishes, synthetic varnishes, and water-latex emulsions. Several easy-to-use products have appeared —one with a toothpaste consistency, a water-latex emulsion, and an aerosol can.

Padding stains, long the antique restorer's secret weapon, are really a form of over-glaze, applied over existing finishes to obtain specific local effects. Shellac or a special padding lacquer is applied to a pad which is dipped into dry, powdered padding colors, then transferred to the surface. It is applied over an older finish—never on the wood—and

rubbed in, to produce the color, pattern, or marking effect desired. As well as being convenient for local color touch-up, this is the home antiquer's best friend for adding visible age to pieces of average value.

Fillers

For a glossy, smooth-finished wood surface, most woods need at least a trace of filler to enable the top coats to completely level out. With woods such as birch and maple, one of the relatively low-solids, brushing-type sanding-filler-sealers can be used. Or, simply rely on rubbed-out, multiple coats of finish to level the surface. Woods at the other end of the pore size scale, such as oak and chest-

MIXING STAIN COLORS

Don't expect a given stain to match your preconception of the color that goes with the name assigned to it. Every stain manufacturer has his own concept of walnut or mahogany colors. However, you can mix stains to match almost any color that you have in mind. If you intend to do much staining, get a selection of the basic wood colors, plus black. Five colors will do the job: black, light oak (yellowish), maple (orange), red mahogany (red), and walnut (basic brown). Starting points for proportions are shown on the following chart:

	Black	Oak (Yellow)	Maple (Orange)	Red Mahogany	Walnut (Brown)	Thinner
Antique Pine				1	4	X
Antique Brown		1	4		12	O
Brown Mahogany		1		1	7	O
Antique Maple		2	5		2	X
Honey Maple		6	3		1	X
Brown Cherry		2		2	3	O
Fruitwood		8	2		1	X
Dark Oak		3			2	O
Modern Walnut	T	5			8	O
Red Cherry				3	2	O

T —Add as desired a drop or so at a time.
X —These need more thinning than most.
O —Test full strength, then dilute to achieve exact intensity desired.

Should you have access to pure color stains, most colors can be mixed from black, dark blue, orange, red, yellow. Since the comparative strengths of dyes differ widely among brands and colors, it is only possible to give a starting point for a proportional listing:

	Black	Dark Blue	Orange	Yellow	Red
Dark Red Mahogany	1		3	1	3
Medium Walnut	3		7		1
Maple		T	5	2	
Golden Oak		T	3	7	

T —Use a touch of these colors as desired.

To mix wiping stains using oil or universal colorants in boiled linseed oil and turpentine (1:3 ratio), use the following quantities as starting points:

	Burnt Umber	Raw Umber	Burnt Sienna	Yellow Ochre	Vermilion
Antique Pine	1	T		1	
Fruitwood	4		5	1	
Oak	2	1		T	
Medium Walnut	2	3		T	
Brown Mahogany	1	1			T
Red Mahogany		1	1		T

T —Use a touch of these colors as desired.

nut, require fairly heavy-bodied "paste" fillers to obtain a level surface.

For the home craftsman, the choice really narrows to sanded-down multiple coats of the top finish (a tedious procedure, except for extremely small-pored woods) and the heavy-bodied silex paste fillers. The low-solids, brush-type sanding-filler-sealer materials tend to cause adhesion problems unless the specific top coat recommended by the sealer manufacturer is used.

There are paste fillers on the market with other than a silex base. Unless you are striving for a special effect which they alone can give, stay with "silex." It's clearer and doesn't shrink and cause dropouts.

In the can, the filler will resemble cream-colored, separated peanut butter. You can buy it in colors, but colors in tubes let you mix-and-match to your own color and quantity specifications. A strong magnifying glass reveals that it consists of finely ground, almost crystalline shards of silex (a finely ground natural flint), suspended in a slightly syrup-like linseed oil or synthetic varnish binder, which requires thorough stirring before and during use.

As purchased, it is far too thick to use and must be thinned with turpentine or other manufacturer-recommended thinner—never with oil—to the consistency of a thick house paint or thick whipping cream (thinning is permissible with finer-pored woods). It should brush well, yet have enough body to fill the wood pores without excess shrinkage through thinner evaporation.

With few exceptions, colors are added to fillers to make them darker than the stained and finished wood. A few specialty finishes, such as silver fox oak (black wood with silver fill), require fillers lighter than wood color. A few finishes use neutral or transparent filler.

Before applying a filler, apply a wash coat of thin shellac (1 part of 4-pound cut shellac to 8 parts denatured alcohol) or a compatible commercial sanding sealer. The wash coat prevents any muddying or staining action by the filler, prevents stain from bleeding into the filler, and smooths and hardens the surface to ease wiping and cleaning. The wash coat MUST be thin enough not to temporarily fill in or bridge the pores, which could prevent proper filling.

To apply filler, use an old short-bristled paint brush or a heavy but cheap brush with about one-fourth of the length of its bristles cut off. Load the brush and scrub it into and with the grain. When you are sure that all pores have some filler in them,

STAIN repaired surface to blend with surrounding area using fine brush to produce grained effect.

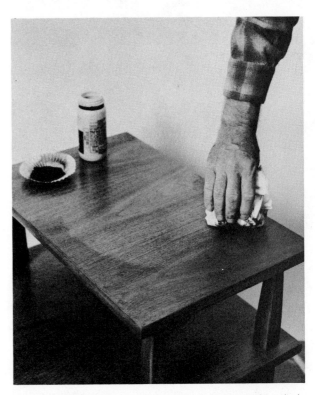

APPLY padding stain powder with cloth dipped in shellac for antiqued effect or to match original color.

start brushing across the grain with a well loaded brush to fill them completely.

The surface will look messy, but wait until the surface has dulled and no longer looks wet. Then start rubbing, slicing, or pressing the excess filler off the surface. The whole point is to remove the excess on the surface without removing or disturbing that part of the filler in the pores.

Three methods of removing filler from the surface are: 1) Rub it off across the grain ONLY with burlap, excelsior, or similar hard-surfaced material. 2) Slice it off with the sharp, straight edge of a wide wall taping knife; thin, stiff cardboard (playing cards work well); or thin, stiff plastic. Then rub as in (1) above. 3) Force it off with the materials in (2) above, then rub. All methods seem to work, and a little experimenting will help you to find your preference.

Trying to rub, slice, or force while the surface is too wet will push the filler out; if the surface is too dry, you will pull the filler out and leave a tacky surface.

Wipe the surface as clean as you can—any filler left will dull and muddy the surface and will have to be sanded later. Let it dry overnight. On very open woods, two or more filler applications may be necessary. When dry, check for any rough or dull spots indicating surface filler. Work these carefully with very fine abrasive paper—well moistened, waterproof paper on a felt pad works well. Cut just deep enough to remove the filler, not deep enough to enter stain and wood, or it will have to be touched up and refilled.

With at least 24 hours drying time, any finish can be put over the filled surface. If you intend to use a top coat material that is new to you or that you suspect may lift the filler, follow the top coat manufacturer's instructions for the filler material and treatment.

WORK FILLER carefully into grain using stiff-bristled brush until all grain is partially filled.

BRUSH ADDITIONAL FILLER across the partially filled grain until grain is completely filled and smooth.

FILLED SURFACE will appear wet and have a paste-like opaque appearance. Allow to dry to dull finish.

REMOVE EXCESS FILLER with a piece of plastic or cardboard using a slicing motion across the grain.

WHICH ABRASIVE TO USE?

Abrasive papers are graded by the size of the cutting grains. Garnet, aluminum oxide and silicon carbide papers use either the standard grit (grain size) numbers (12 through 600) or an "O" number (1/0, 2/0, 3/0, 4/0, etc.), grain size designation, or both. Emery, sand, or flint papers are graded similarly.

Papers less densely coated with grit are called open coat papers. They cut slower and clog less than standard papers.

Paper backings for abrasive papers are graded A, C, D, and E. A is the most flexible, E the least flexible. Waterproof backings are also available for wet sanding.

Cloth backings are available in jeans, drills, and combinations. Jeans is a lightweight blue denim material, drills is medium weight, and combinations are stiff, heavy duty materials.

The most often used grit sizes and their uses are listed in the chart below. Hardwoods are best sanded with each listed grade in sequence. Any time apparently saved by skipping a grit size or two may be lost because of the extra time necessary to smooth out sanding marks made by the previous coarser grit size. Softwoods (pine, fir, spruce, redwood, etc.), can be satisfactorily smoothed by using only those grades marked by an asterisk.

INTENDED USE	GRIT NUMBER	RECOMMENDED BACKING GUIDE	"O" SERIES NUMBER
Gross surface removal, shaping and leveling.	80*	D	1/0
Initial smoothing steps.	100*	C	2/0
	120	A or C	3/0
Intermediate smoothing steps, often skipped by do-it-yourselfers, but which are worth using when aiming for the fastest route to the finest finish.	150*	A	4/0
	180	A	5/0
Fine smoothing on wood surfaces.	220*	A	6/0
Final sanding on the harder, denser woods, and for between coat level sanding and scuffing of finish coats.	240	A	7/0
	280	A	8/0
	320	A	9/0
Wet sanding—using water, thinner or oils—on finish top coats to obtain eggshell or semi-gloss surface.	360	Waterproof	
	400	Waterproof	10/0
	500	Waterproof	11/0
	600	Waterproof	12/0

Your Choices in Wood Finishes

Wood finishes are marketed with a variety of names, chemical constituents, and containers. Surprisingly, though, they begin to fall into fairly well defined groups when you take a close look at 1) the method of hardening, 2) solvent content, 3) resin content, 4) whether they are clear or opaque, and 5) whether they form a surface layer or penetrate and harden in the wood.

Those that harden primarily by oxidation of the vehicle oils are oleoresinous varnishes. Those that harden primarily by evaporation of solvents are spirit varnishes or modern lacquers. Those that harden by catalytic action are the ultramodern tough catalytic coatings.

A quick breakdown of solvent identifications reveals that an alcohol solvent indicates shellac; lacquer thinner indicates any of the modern cellulose, vinyl, acrylic, or related lacquers; and turpentine or "paint thinner" indicates any of the several oleoresinous or synthetic varnishes.

The resin content often names the product, as in shellac, dammar, and copal. In other instances, pairing the resin with its solvent helps identify the category. Thus, vinyl resin with a lacquer thinner solvent indicates a vinyl lacquer, but vinyl resin with water as a clean-up solvent indicates a vinyl emulsion or latex product.

Pronounced opacity indicates that a finish is probably lacquer, natural resin, or a synthetic resin varnish vehicle with pigments and/or dyes added.

Surface penetrants usually contain a high percentage of solvents for greater ease of penetration. Surface films can be in any category.

Common to all finishes are the requirements that the wood surfaces must be properly prepared with bleach, stain, seal, and filler as required; and that all waxes, grease, or dirt must be removed from the surface.

Oil Finishes

The hard oil finish has, for all practical purposes, been upstaged by more durable, easily applied and maintained modern penetrating resin finishes. However, the almost legendary character of oil finishes requires a brief mention for those who may have a specific need for it.

Boiled linseed oil mixed 1:1 with distilled spirits of turpentine is heated over a double boiler away from flame to about 80 degrees Fahrenheit. The mixture should be heated with great care, as it is flammable.

Wet the wood surface thoroughly with the hot oil mixture and allow it to soak in. Wipe the surface free of visible oil. Repeat several times the first day, then once daily for a week, weekly for a month, and monthly for a year. The dry surface should be polished for at least an hour between applications.

An early American variation calls for keeping the surface wet with the oil mixture for a day or two

LACQUER FINISH of buffet was rubbed with pumice and rubbing oil to produce low-gloss, satiny surface.

until the surface absorbs no more. Then pumice powder is sprinkled on the surface and rubbed vigorously with a burlap pad. All traces of pumice should be removed after rubbing. Repeat pumice rub three times, with the oil mixture twice and pure linseed oil the third time. A final rottenstone and oil rub will produce a higher gloss if desired. Finally, wax with a hard paste wax. Re-oil every year or two.

A slightly more modern version calls for equal parts boiled linseed oil, spirits of turpentine, and spar varnish. The mixture is applied and rubbed vigorously with a moistened, lint-free cloth pad. The rubbing should continue until the surface appears unable to absorb more mixture. Wring the pad dry and rub the surface until no signs of wetness appear on the surface. Repeat the process at weekly intervals until the surface pleases you. Wait a week and apply the first of several weekly paste floor wax polishings. Repeat wax polishing at least twice a year thereafter.

These techniques produce beautiful initial results, but unless you are willing to devote much time and energy to maintenance, all too often surfaces soon pick up dirt and dust.

Penetrating Resin Finishes

Everyone dreams of a finish so simple to apply that brushes and brush marks are banished—a finish that flows on as simply as "washing" and provides a tough, resilient surface that resists impact, abrasion, stain, chemical, heat, and water.

If you like the natural wood look and texture, without the "wood under glass" look of on-the-surface finishes, you have found your product in penetrating resin finishes which beautify the wood surface without calling attention to themselves.

Penetrating finishes soak into the surface of the wood to surround the wood fibers and fill much of the cell structure near the surface. Thus they use the wood structure as the fibrous filler for a plastic surface similar in many respects to the plastic laminates used for boats and sports car bodies—but with the warmth, texture, and beauty of natural wood.

The resins provide a slight darkening effect that greatly enhances the grain and figure and develops the fire and color of the wood.

All you need is a surface sanded smooth, free of grease and wax and vacuumed clear of sanding dust; and a can of any of the many brands of penetrating resin finish.

Apply enough resin with a cloth pad, brush, or 2/0 steel wool swab to keep the surface wet for at least half an hour, often longer depending on specific manufacturer's recommendations. Add more resin if the surface dulls before the wet period is over. At the end of the wet or soak period, use clean rags (preferably old and lint-free) to wipe the surface clear of all resin. Watch the surface for small spots of resin which are often forced to the surface by heat or air bubbles and wipe the surface completely dry.

Second and third soaks, 24 hours apart, are well worth the effort if the wood will absorb more resin. The more resin absorbed—with no surface coating—the tougher the finish and the harder the surface will be.

If, by chance, some resin starts to harden on the surface and resists normal rag wipe-up, moisten a pad of 2/0 steel wool in liquid resin and gently rub and allow to set up for at least 24 hours between steps.

After the final treatment you will have as nearly indestructible a finish as you can apply. If the surface is scratched or marred, merely apply more resin to the area to subdue the scratches or marring by blending the color to the original.

Experimenting on scrap lumber will illustrate that penetrating resins are at their best on the darker and more porous woods (rosewood, teak, walnut, oak, cherry, mahogany, and lauan). The lighter colored woods show the least color development.

If you prefer a slightly heavier body to the finish, use one of the penetrating resin floor finishes. Apply it as directed for the first coat, then add up to 25 per cent of the same manufacturer's best compatible floor varnish to the next several coats until the pore fill is to your liking. Use a fist-sized pad—such as used in French polishing—to apply the fortified mixture. Rub it in with a circular motion across the grain until evenly coated, then pad gently but firmly with the grain until any unevenness or blemishes are removed. Dry thoroughly, at least overnight. Smooth with 220-grit open-coat abrasive paper, clean with 2/0 steel wool, and vacuum.

Repeat until desired surface is obtained, then rub down with 2/0, 3/0, and 4/0 steel wool—with the grain. The final rub may be with a hard-surface, floor-type paste wax. Allow the wax to harden for 10 to 15 minutes, then buff with the grain with a tampico fiber brush. A flannel or felt pad can be used after the brush for a higher polish.

Quick "Oil" Finish

Most of us get the urge to duplicate the old time hard oil finishes but dread the long term work involved. If that is the case, simply use a good penetrating resin finish as directed. Then, when the resin has dried for at least 5 days, rub in warm boiled linseed oil then rub off excess to achieve the odor and very slight tactile drag associated with hard oiled surfaces.

Experiment first on an inconspicuous spot. The resin may not darken the surface to an oil finished color. If necessary you can wipe the raw wood surface with boiled linseed oil for color development, let dry for 72 hours, then continue with the penetrating resin finish.

Shellac Finishes

Shellac was the chosen finish until the advent of modern oleoresinous varnishes and synthetic lacquers at the turn of the century.

There is no other finish that can give the particular deep, liquid-fire effect to the colors, grains, and figures of many of the medium and dark cabinet woods and veneers.

It was the first and, for decades, the only finish that could be rubbed to a finish approaching the fabled Oriental lacquers. The original "piano" finish was actually a clear or pigmented shellac rubbed to a perfect gloss or eggshell.

Its qualities of good adhesion to wood, flexibility, clarity, impact, and abrasion resistance have kept it alive far longer than its apparent disadvantages would seem to indicate. It is still considered a good finish for dry, high gloss, wooden floors.

Shellac's disadvantages have to do with its solubility. It is soluble in too many liquids in common use. To varying degrees, it is soluble in lacquer thinners, alcohols and related solvents (nail polish and martinis), alkaline solutions such as ammonia and strong soaps and detergents, and even hard water. Furniture finished in shellac needs to be retouched frequently, and this decreases its popularity in most homes.

However, for a quick, clear, fast drying (in minutes because of the alcohol solvent), glossy finish that can be successfully applied by brush, shellac is excellent. It is especially good if it is to be used on decorative pieces that will not be exposed to solvents or cocktails. Scratches, abrasions, and most blemishes usually can be repaired by applying alcohol or new shellac.

Shellac should *ALWAYS* be purchased fresh and only in quantities needed for a particular project. Shellac deteriorates in storage, so select a store with good turnover and fresh stock. Any stored shellac should be tested on scrap wood. If it dries normally to a hard, tack-free surface, then it is suitable for use. Shellac that dries gummy will remain that way in use.

Both white and orange shellacs are available; the prime difference is the color effect on the wood surface.

There is no successful one-coat shellac finish, but the rapid drying (dries dust-free in 15 to 30 minutes and is recoatable in 2 to 4 hours, depending on penetration, humidity, and shellac consistency) and almost foolproof recoatability make shellac the easiest of all surface finishes to apply. As the solvents in liquid shellac soften dry shellac surfaces, the blending and adhesion of overlaps and successive layers are virtually perfect.

If you have never worked with shellac before, start off with a 1-pound cut—it is the shellac consistency that is most forgiving of mistakes. As you grow more experienced, you can work with the heavier consistencies of 3-pound cuts.

After smoothing, staining, and filling, use a fully loaded brush to apply a wet coat of shellac with a slow, smooth-flowing motion to overlap adjoining strokes and develop a clean, bubble- and void-free film.

Allow the first coat of shellac to dry thoroughly, usually 1 to 2 hours. Sand smooth using a felt or rubber-backed block and 180 to 220-grit open-coated garnet or aluminum oxide paper or the white, filled, no-load silicon carbide papers. Any shellac-clogged paper can be washed and brushed out with shellac thinner, dried, and re-used. Flint paper can be used, but the crude, relatively inflexible paper backing, short cutting life, and grit dropout problems make it untrustworthy.

Repeat the shellac application and sanding a second time.

The third coat should look smooth and level; if not, resand it. If it is smooth but needs rubbing to achieve an eggshell or flat waxable surface, use 4/0 steel wool or FFF pumice with rubbing oil and a felt pad. In both cases, rub with the grain, and rub out any glassy spots. If pumice and oil are used, wash the surface with a dilute acid solution (1:1 vinegar and water) or rub it down with cornstarch to remove all oil.

If a high-gloss finish is desired, follow the pumice and oil rub, after a three-day hardening period, with a rottenstone and rubbing oil rub. Rub until the surface has an overall high polish. Clean and dry as for the pumice rub.

If the surface is to be waxed, wait 24 hours after the last surface treatment and apply a hard paste wax, buffing as directed.

French Polish

This is a shellac finishing process that dominated from the time of Louis XIV through the Chippendale, Sheraton, and Hepplewhite designs. No other finish can equal the tough, velvety sheen achieved by thin multiple coats of shellac.

After smoothing, staining, and cleaning, rub the surface down with boiled linseed oil and dry thoroughly. While the oiled surface is drying, prepare a French polishing pad. It should have a firm, resilient cloth center about which is wrapped a lint-free material—usually cotton or old linen. Virtually every finisher has his own recipe for a French polishing pad, from silk stockings to mechanic's waste for the center, and from cotton flannel to linen tablecloths for the outer cover. Basically, make a conical wad for the center, set it in the middle of a 6-inch square cover cloth, and bring the corners of the cover up over the top.

Saturate the pad with ¾ to 1-pound cut shellac by squeezing and releasing until the pad is evenly moist but not dripping. Place a drop or two of raw linseed oil on the pad and start rubbing the surface with a non-stop motion until the pad no

---

WHEN YOU CHOOSE A SHELLAC...

Shellac consistency is defined in terms of cut. For example, a 4-pound cut is 4 pounds of dry shellac resin dissolved in 1 gallon of denatured alcohol.

Because few stores carry dry resin, your best bet is to start with one of the standard 3-, 4-, or 5-pound cuts that are sold commercially, then make the consistency you desire by use of the chart below.

Always use shellac thinner grade alcohol.

DESIRED CONSISTENCY		COMMERCIALLY AVAILABLE CONSISTENCY DESIGNATED AS POUNDS CUT (POUND CUT)					
		3-Pound Cut		4-Pound Cut		5-Pound Cut	
Consistency	Cut	Alcohol	Shellac	Alcohol	Shellac	Alcohol	Shellac
Very Thin	½-pound	4 Parts	1 Part	5 Parts	1 Part	7 Parts	1 Part
Fairly Thin	1-pound	4 Parts	3 Parts	3 Parts	1 Part	2 Parts	1 Part
Thin	1½-pound	3 Parts	4 Parts	3 Parts	2½ Parts	1½ Parts	1 Part
Medium	2-pound	2 Parts	5 Parts	3 Parts	4 Parts	1 Part	1 Part
Fairly Medium	2½-pound	1 Part	5 Parts	1 Part	2 Parts	2 Parts	3 Parts
Thick	3-pound		Full strength	1 Part	4 Parts	1 Part	2 Parts
Fairly Thick	4-pound				Full strength	1 Part	4 Parts
Very Thick	5-pound						Full strength

longer deposits shellac. Without stopping the circular motion, remove the pad. Add more shellac and a drop or two of oil and start the circular motion in the air before touching the surface. Even momentary stops on the surface have a tendency to gum the surface. Keep rubbing until the surface is completely covered. Allow the surface to dry 24 hours.

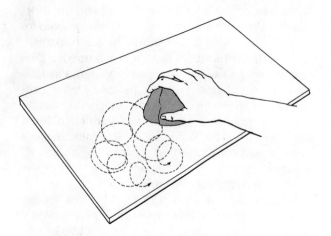

Repeat the French polish rub daily until the surface meets your approval. A final coat can be added a week later for maximum polish if desired. Allow 24 hours final drying time, then remove oil by one of three methods. The traditional one, called spiriting off, involves using a clean pad wet with denatured alcohol, wringing it dry, and quickly wiping across the surface in a circular polishing motion. The second calls for moistening the entire surface using a turpentine-soaked pad, then sprinkling either rottenstone or pumice—depending on the degree of polish or eggshell desired—evenly over the entire surface. Use a soft, shoe-polishing-type brush to stroke parallel to the grain until all the turpentine is taken up by the powder. A final wipe with the grain, using a soft cotton rag, will reveal an oil-free finish buffed to perfection.

The third method is to wipe with a turpentine-soaked rag and polish dry.

The fourth method adds a 1:1 vinegar and water washing of the surface after first wiping with turpentine.

A short cut to producing French polish is to brush or pad regular 1½-pound shellac on the surface in as many coats as desired. Sand-level between coats with 4/0 to 6/0 abrasive paper. Apply the final coat by French polish. The finish is almost as clear as the real thing, and a lot faster!

When repairing or adding another coat, be sure to have the pad in motion before touching the surface.

Lacquer Finishes

Modern lacquer is a fast-drying synthetic finish which, like shellac, hardens through evaporation of highly volatile solvents. Lacquer was first created in a search for a fast-drying substitute for varnish, which took too long to dry, and shellac, which was

---

RUBBING MATERIALS AND TECHNIQUES

Rubbing with pumice or rottenstone is merely a means of controlled abrading of the surface to produce an even matte or polished surface. Pumice usually is available in three grades—F, FF, and FFF. Unless otherwise specified, use FFF—the finest grade—whenever pumice is called for. Drug stores sometimes carry their own version of FFF pumice for tooth polishing compounds. Rottenstone generally is available only in a single grade. It is finely ground, decomposed, siliceous limestone, and has the faint odor of rotten eggs.

Rubbing lubricants are always used with pumice and rottenstone. When rubbing oil is called for, use light mineral oil, paraffin oil, *raw* linseed, or the so-called "lemon" or "almond" oils (actually mineral oil with lemon or almond essence added).

Water can be used alone or with mild soap if called for. A particularly good soap is the linsfoot, or linseed soap. *Never* use water as the lubricant with shellac.

The powders sometimes are mixed with the lubricant to form a slurry of a creamy consistency.

Many workers prefer to wet the surface thoroughly, then sprinkle the powders from a large salt shaker over the surface. Rub with a layer or two of hard felt (from a man's hat) glued to a block of wood, or a hard felt block obtainable from some paint stores or mail order houses. Keep pumice and rottenstone blocks separated. Pumice on the rottenstone block ruins it for use.

Always rub with the grain. Minor imperfections paralleling the grain are much less visible than those that cross the grain.

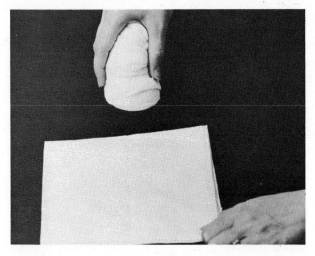

WIND GAUZE or cheesecloth into conical-shaped core large enough to fit comfortably into your hand.

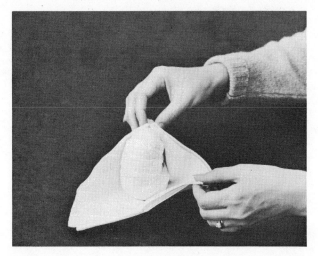

WRAP CORE with piece of lint-free cotton or linen. Well-washed handkerchiefs, table linens work well.

SATURATE PAD with 1-pound cut shellac (see page 37). Squeeze until drip free, add 3-4 drops linseed oil.

RUB SHELLAC onto the surface with a gentle circular motion until a thin, even coating is applied.

SPRINKLE DRY PUMICE or rottenstone over the final dry coat of shellac, buff with soft brush.

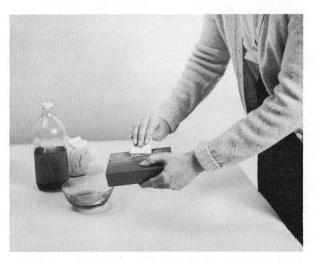

WASH DRY SURFACE with a mixture of vinegar and water (equal parts) to remove any oil residue.

too sensitive to heat, alcohol, and water. Today, lacquer for all practical purposes replaces both shellac and varnish on factory produced furniture. Lacquers represent the thinnest coating of all on-the-surface finishes.

Most lacquers are extremely fast-drying and are intended for spray application. This high drying speed, often in minutes, is probably the main reason lacquers have such a poor reputation among home-craftsmen.

There are, however, several good brushing lacquers on the market, although they are seldom identified as such. Also, several manufacturers have started selling special drying retarders so that their spray lacquers can be brushed. Brushing-type floor lacquers are probably the most widely available and, with care, are satisfactory for craft use.

No matter what lacquer you buy, get enough thinner *BY THE SAME MANUFACTURER* to complete the job. While most thinners appear the same, there are sufficient differences to cause drying, adhesion, and blemish troubles in some cases.

Spray can lacquers are fine for small areas and can be used to build up a multi-layered finish. For multi-coating with level sanding between, wait at least four hours between coats. Lacquer solvents are so efficient that the smallest trace of solvent in a lower coat may allow the top coat's solvent to penetrate too deeply and soften the lower layers with resulting wrinkles, sags, and pin holes. The ultimate damage is having the entire surface soften to such an extent that it oozes off.

Lacquer solvents dissolve natural dyes in several woods, notably rosewood, amaranth, and mahogany. Many spirit and oil stains and fillers are either dissolved or softened and lifted into the lacquer layer. Lacquer-compatible products should be used whenever possible. They include N.G.R. stains, lacquer-safe fillers, and lacquer-shielding wash coats—usually shellac or lacquer sanding-sealer. If noncompatible products are used, be sure to allow a minimum of 48 hours drying time for all steps, and use shellac or lacquer sanding-sealer as a wash coat under the lacquer.

HOW TO MAKE AND USE A TACK RAG

Tack rags, available at most paint stores, are an indispensable part of the finisher's anti-dust arsenal. Use the varnish-tacky (but not sticky) cloths to lightly wipe any surface prior to finish coating.

Usually tack rags are made of cheesecloth. You can make your own from a well washed, lint-free cotton cloth, heavy cheesecloth, discarded oxford-cloth shirt, or diaper. Dip the cloth in lukewarm water and wring out; then thoroughly wet with turpentine and wring out. Lay the cloth out on a clean surface and drip varnish on the surface until it is well spotted. Fold two edges in to the center, then roll and wring tightly. Repeat the wringing, and roll between the hands until the cloth, when opened, is uniformly coated.

The cloth should pick up and hold dust but leave no residue when you wipe surfaces with it. Keep the rag in a sealed jar, and periodically restore it by application of very small amounts of water and turpentine.

WRING OUT piece of soft material or cheesecloth dipped in warm water.

SATURATE CLOTH with turpentine; squeeze until it is drip free.

SCATTER DROPS of varnish onto rag, knead cloth until it is evenly tacky.

Use a wide, moderately full brush to flow a continuous, wet coat onto the surface with minimum of retrace or back brushing—preferably none. Work areas small enough so that by working with long, fast, continuous strokes you can keep each succeeding stroke working against the wet edge of the last stroke.

Work only clean surfaces. The fast, dust-free drying won't help if there is dust and grit on the surface. A dry tack rag moving ahead of the brush is a help.

Until you become familiar with lacquer, work with lacquer thinned down slightly—just enough so that it flows and levels well from the brush. Allow it to dry for at least two, preferably four hours. Sand with 4/0 to 6/0 paper only if necessary to remove defects and level the surface. Clean, vacuum, and dry-tack-rag the surface; then add the next coat.

Repeat coats if necessary, with at least four to six hours drying time between coats. The final coat may be rubbed with pumice and/or rottenstone in rubbing oil.

For spray application, refer to page 75 and the manufacturer's instructions on the lacquer and spray equipment. There are enough differences in sprayers to make reference to the manufacturer's instructions mandatory.

Lacquer finishes offer advantages in speedy, dust-free drying, fast multiple coating, clarity, and hardness. Lacquer also darkens wood the least of all the finishes. This last characteristic is especially true of the filled lacquer lighteners that leave the wood almost at its sanded color.

Varnish Finishes

Fine modern varnishes produce a full-bodied, tough finish that is heat, abrasion, impact, chemical, alcohol, and water-resistant. They are by far the most durable and protective of all the clear, on-the-surface finishes.

To some, the loss of most of the old natural resin varnishes is considered a catastrophe, but with few exceptions the loss is a blessing for the home craftsman. The problem was that natural resins weren't tailored to any specific job. To compound the problem, many people believed that traditional long oil spar varnish was the best varnish. But spar varnish was designed *NEVER* to completely harden and for that reason is not used on furniture.

Modern synthetic resin varnishes can be tailored to meet specific situations by changing or mixing

---

DUPLICATING ORIENTAL LACQUERS

Duplicating Oriental lacquer with the original materials—the sap of the *Rhus verniciflua* and *Toxicodendron vernicifluum*—is difficult, since the trees, if you can find them, have to be chopped up to extract the sap.

However, an approximation to Oriental lacquer can be made with modern automotive lacquers applied in many layers. Dull red (to duplicate the famed cinnabar lacquers), black, and multi-color layers with metal leaf or bronze powder inclusions all can be used. After building up sufficient layers, abrade or carve and polish down to lower metallic or colored layers. Use the thinnest possible supporting material, and coat both sides equally or you will risk severe warping. After working the surface, polish and recoat with clear lacquer.

If you attempt the deeply carved version, you will need at least 100 coats of lacquer, with at least four to eight hours drying time and level sanding between coats.

---

resins to achieve precise differences in flexibility, hardness, clarity, scuff resistance, and chemical or water resistance, without depending on natural oil-resin combinations.

Best of all, synthetic resin varnishes generally are easier to apply, last longer, and produce better surfaces than the oil-resin finishes.

The three basic synthetics readily available to the craftsman are alkyd, phenolic, and urethane. Don't be surprised to see acrylics, vinyls, polyurethanes, silicones, epoxies, and others. They are all becoming available. A water emulsion, clear varnish has been test marketed.

A good protective varnish coating is fairly easy to apply. Simply apply with no voids, on a clean surface, and dry thoroughly before recoating.

Unfortunately, achieving a visually attractive varnish coating is something of a problem. Since varnishes dry or set up more slowly than any other major finish category, they also suffer from serious dust problems. However, in a reasonably dust-free room and with judicious between-coat sanding and final coat rubbing, beautiful level finishes can be obtained.

As dust is a problem, craftsmen have developed two methods of reducing the problem of dust, lint, bristle, and hair particles. The simplest method, requiring the least preparation but not always too effective, is to moisten and point an extremely fine

PICKING STICK HEAD is made by dipping tip of thin wire or sliver of wood into a heated mixture of varnish and powdered or block rosin. Tap head against palm of hand until it becomes very tacky.

artist's brush between the lips and use the sharp point to lift the dust straight up and out of the surface film.

A favorite dust remover is the picking stick, having a pear-shaped mass of a sticky "burnt varnish" on one end. "Burnt varnish" is prepared by heating one part varnish to approximately eight parts of crushed or powdered rosin. Add the rosin slowly, stirring constantly with a wooden stick, until a drop of the melted mix forms a stiff, gummy, taffy-candy-like pill when dropped on a cool ceramic or glass plate. Prepare it in small quantities over indirect heat only. A miniature double boiler consisting of a small orange juice can in a pineapple-slice can works well. If your local paint or hardware store can't supply the brown rosin, go to a sports store for a rosin bag or to a music store for a block of bow rosin.

To use the rosin-varnish mixture, dip the tip of the stick into the cooling mixture and withdraw a small ball, preferably not over an eighth of an inch in diameter. Use moistened fingers to shape the ball to a pear shape—saliva is the most convenient and most effective finger moistener. Then gently roll and tap the pear-shaped ball in the palm of your hand until it feels sticky.

Lower it, with a gentle tapping motion, on the dust, lint, bristle, or hair, and withdraw it vertically. Never attempt varnishing in the same workroom

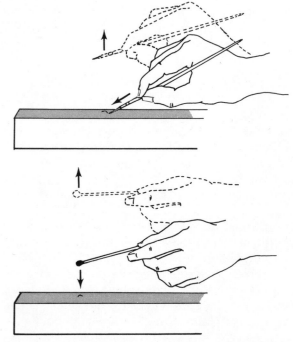

REMOVE DUST SPOT with tip of fine brush or use picking stick that has a tacky varnish head.

where general woodworking or sanding is performed. Use a room that can be virtually sealed off from traffic and drafts. A spare bedroom often works well with a paper or plastic tarpaulin on the floor. Place the item to be varnished and all equipment in the room, vacuum room and contents well, close room and let remaining dust settle for several hours.

Some workers spray with a fine mist of water or use a vaporizer to load the air with moisture, thus capturing flying dust. Then they vacuum up the settled dust and allow the air to dry out. Begin varnish preparations by using the tack rag to remove any dust from the work surfaces—work the tack rag ahead of the varnish brush. Don't miss any dust, it will cause trouble later.

Fill a clean varnish cup about half full of clear varnish. If the varnish has been open for some time or if you suspect it may have become seedy with granules of hardened varnish, filter it through several layers of clean, discarded nylon stocking or several layers of fine cheesecloth. Dip the filter material in shellac, stretch and dry it to "encapsulate" any stray fibers that could muddy the varnish.

Dip a clean, high quality varnish brush about a third (never more than two-thirds) of its bristle length in the varnish. Lightly draw it across the strike wire of the varnish cup to remove bubbles and excess varnish. Don't squeeze it across the wire, as squeezing removes too much varnish, deforms the brush bristles, and wastes effort.

Start applying the varnish as evenly and smoothly as possible with fast continuous strokes. Plan your work so that the start of your stroke is at an unvarnished point. It is difficult to start a brush stroke in a wet area without leaving "stab" marks and it is easier to float the brush up and off when ending a stroke in a wet area. Before any area can start to set up, dry the brush by drawing it across the strike wire, then lightly tip off any bubbles, brush marks, or runs.

Many professionals play a game of tic-tac-toe. Try this method on a scrap surface with full-strength varnish. If absolutely necessary, for ease of brushing or faster surface leveling, add the smallest—the very smallest—amount of pure-distilled spirits of turpentine or the specific thinner recommended by the varnish manufacturer. Stir slowly but completely, let the mixture stand for an hour or two, and stir gently before using, allowing any bubbles to settle out. The wrong thinner can "curdle" many synthetic varnishes. An alternate thinning method is to heat the varnish in a hot water bath, to not more than 140° F, before applying.

DIP BRUSH into varnish cup. Wipe off excess by drawing brush across wire inserted in top of can.

Lay down three or more full brush-width bands of varnish parallel to the long dimension of the piece, spacing them a brush width apart.

Brush across the original varnish bands to achieve an even varnish coat between the bands. Dry off the brush by drawing across the strike wire. Then tip off the varnish in the direction of the original brush strokes with a final tip-off from new to old varnish to level any edges or runs between the two.

Repeat the "tic-tac-toe" technique until the surface is covered.

Try to work all surfaces to be varnished in a horizontal position if possible. It pays off in fewer runs and sags.

Work facing a window or light wall. This lightens the surface reflection and simplifies the location of dry spots, sags, runs, and other defects. A movable stand light serves the same purpose at night.

Use a thinned varnish (1 part distilled spirits of turpentine or specified thinner to 4 parts varnish) as the surface sealer coat for varnish unless you particularly need the color imparted by a thinned shellac sealer coat. Shellac works well under many varnishes, but many urethane-base varnishes don't adhere well on shellac undercoats.

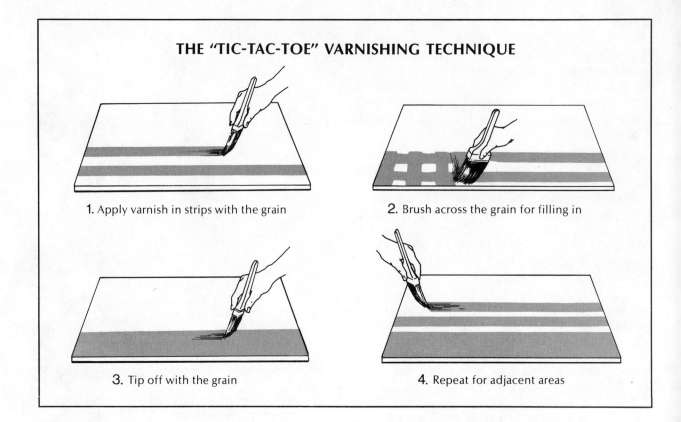

THE "TIC-TAC-TOE" VARNISHING TECHNIQUE

1. Apply varnish in strips with the grain

2. Brush across the grain for filling in

3. Tip off with the grain

4. Repeat for adjacent areas

If you don't catch dry spots, runs, sags, or other potential blemishes while tipping off in a particular area, forget them until the surface is hardened. Sand them level and build up with the next coat. Any rebrushing of a partially set area only leads to problems.

For the best varnish finish, always, unless specifically instructed otherwise by the manufacturer, allow at least 48 hours between varnish coats. Many experienced custom varnishers insist on 72 hours and longer. Varnishes become progressively harder and less gummy over the early days of their lives, and the harder the surface, the better sanding and rubbing job you can do.

Always scuff between varnish coats, even if smoothing or leveling is not needed. New varnish doesn't take well to a glossy surface. There are a few specialty varnishes which adhere best to unsanded surfaces, if recoated within the four to six hour period. If you miss the specified time period, wait at least 24 hours, then scuff and recoat.

Level off each coat with block-mounted sandpaper. Remove "nibs" or "whiskers." Sand enough to completely dull the surface. Leave no shiny areas unless the areas are so recessed that cutting through the finish is required to reach them. If they are that deep, you will have to build up the low areas with successive varnish applications over the whole area, then sand to a common level.

If level sanding on early coats leaves a few glossy depressions, and you decide to proceed, scuff the depressions with 4/0 steel wool.

Repeat coating, sand level to completely dull the surface and, if necessary, rub bright depressions with steel wool. Repeat until you are satisfied with the surface level.

Rub with FFF pumice, rubbing oil, and a felt pad. Coat the surface with a thin layer of oil and sprinkle pumice lightly over the oily surface. Using a felt rubbing pad, rub parallel to the grain until the entire surface is velvet-like and uniformly smooth. The side of your thumb, hand, or a soft rubber block helps in moving the pumice-and-oil aside for a look at the surface.

For a finer gloss, completely clean the surface of pumice-and-oil and use a rottenstone-and-oil rubbing mixture. Be certain that you remove all traces of the pumice, for one or two grains of it can ruin the soft glow resulting from the rottenstone polish. Use a clean felt rubbing pad, reserved for rottenstone only. Rub until examination of the surface shows an almost glass-smooth surface.

Paste wax applied over the varnish surface, a day or two after the last rub and cleanup, will preserve

PUMICE- AND OIL-RUBBING METHOD

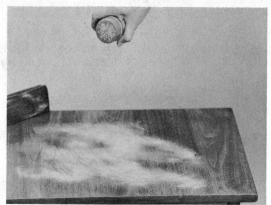

SPRINKLE PUMICE over surface coated with thin film of rubbing oil (an old salt shaker works well).

RUB PUMICE across surface with felt block or blackboard eraser. Clean small area to check results.

ABRASIVE-PAPER RUBBING PROCEDURE

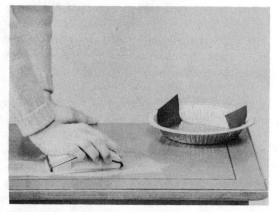

USE WATER and waterproofed abrasive paper (400-grit or finer) for similar effect of a pumice rub.

SPREAD WHITING or talcum powder on surface, rub with fine abrasive paper for coarser pumice-like rub.

WAX APPLICATION AND POLISH

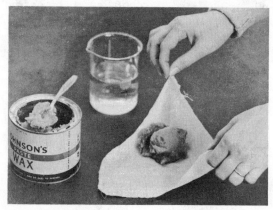

WRAP PASTE WAX in moist rag or sock to make applicator for a thin wax film coating.

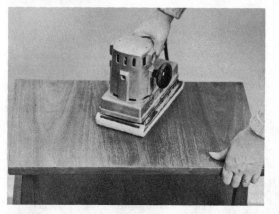

POLISH WAXED SURFACE with felt or lambskin pads. Attach pad to disc sander for quicker results.

the glossy finish. Apply a good hard (preferably carnauba wax) paste-type floor wax as directed, then buff by hand or machine. Handle disc-type buffers carefully. Keep the buffer in constant motion over the surface. A pad-type sander with a lamb's wool or felt polishing pad is slower, but it is safer unless you are experienced with a rotary buffer.

For less exacting finishes, you can use waterproof abrasive papers, 400-grit and finer with either oil or water to produce almost the same effect as with the pumice rub.

The use of waterproof papers for the leveling and polishing of varnish is worth the added cost of the paper, since such papers are extremely flexible and do not clog when wet. If you are working on a large project, start sanding with waterproof paper of a given grit in pairs. That is, keep a spare soaking while you work with one on the block or sander, so that you can make a quick change.

When time is an important factor and where water or oil sanding is troublesome, you might experiment with fine talcum powder as a lubricant under fine, dry, abrasive paper for leveling thoroughly dry finishes. It is easy to brush aside to see the surface and is satisfactory for work that is not too critical.

There is a tendency for many people to use the modern semi-gloss or flat varnishes instead of rubbing down standard glossy varnishes. Where the ultimate varnish finish is not necessary, semi-gloss and flat varnishes provide acceptable surfaces.

Semi-glosses and flat varnishes because of "flattening" additives are not as clear as full-gloss varnishes and should never be used more than two coats thick—preferably one coat on top of glossy varnish. More than one or two coats will degrade the clarity of the wood pattern and color. Unless you have exceptional dust and lint control in your work area, you will probably have dust and lint inclusion in the surface that will have to be rubbed out anyway, thus robbing the low gloss varnishes of any real advantages.

Enamel Finishes

The word "enamel," in modern usage, covers a broad category of materials used for finishes to provide color and covering characteristics. Thus, you will find side by side on a dealer's shelf products called enamels which contain pigments in alkyd varnish base, lacquer base, urethane catalytic varnish base, and many others.

Confusion over enamel selection can be reduced effectively if you recall the characteristics of the related clear finish of the base and match those characteristics to your requirements when you make your choice. With few exceptions, exactly the same procedures, advantages, and limitations apply to a given enamel that apply to its related clear finish except that surface color is not a factor.

You seldom have to fill the wood pores when using enamel undercoats because they are usually heavy in pigment. Normally, a close-grained wood is selected for enameling, since most of the open-grained cabinet woods (mahogany, oak, and walnut) are usually not painted or enameled except as a last resort.

An enamel undercoat is recommended to seal and fill the smoothed wood surface. For large enameling projects, undercoating lowers the first coat cost and facilitates the acceptance of the enamel top coat. The undercoat is usually white and should be tinted to approach the color of the top coat, or you will never achieve a one-coat top coat of a darker enamel. As undercoating means extra material, application, and cleanup steps, it can be a long-term saving on a large project, but when enameling a small unpainted chair, chest, or end table for example, can be inconvenient.

Thinned enamel itself makes a good prime coat although it does not work too well as a filler. Thin 4 parts of enamel to 1 part of the specific solvent recommended on the can, and apply as you would a sealer coat of the parent material, lacquer or varnish.

When looking for an enamel to do a particularly

COMPLETE SCUFFING PROCESS by removing bright spots with 4/0 steel wool or 400-grit abrasive papers.

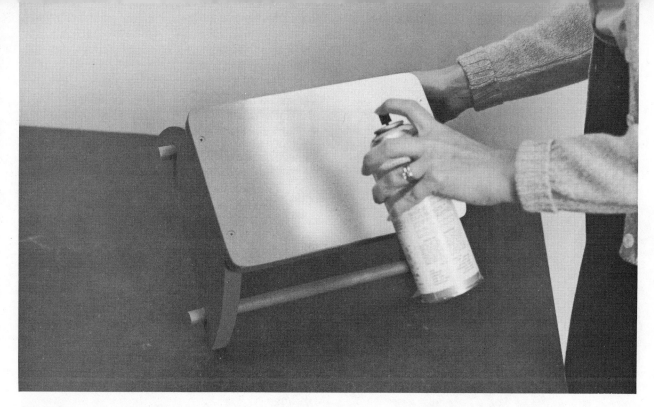

SPRAY ENAMELS are good for use on children's furniture where retouching is constantly required. Spray quickly and evenly to assure a smooth and complete coverage over the entire area.

fine finishing project, consider the lacquer and enamel-based automotive finishes. They come in an array of colors, tints, and tones usually unmatched in the regular paint and enamel lines.

As with varnishes, enamels come in glossy, semi-glossy, and flat finishes. The flat enamel is often paintlike in its flatness. Glossy enamel is the most durable with the less glossy enamels being less durable.

For a fine finish, a well rubbed glossy enamel is more beautiful and durable than the more convenient low-gloss enamel finishes. However, low-gloss enamels can be used to advantage where an extremely fine finish is not required.

A further advantage of the glossy enamels is that they usually are available in darker color tones. Dark color tones can be lightened by adding lighter glossy enamels, whereas light semi-gloss or flat enamels can only be darkened by adding pigment (a color-mixing device at the paint store helps with the mixing) with attendant higher cost and probable loss of durability. Drying time also is increased because of the increased pigment-to-resin ratio.

If you do decide on a semi-gloss enamel top coat, a full-gloss enamel gives a much faster (fewer coats) and more durable buildup for the undercoats.

Spray all lacquer-based enamels, as a brushing lacquer-based enamel is rare. If you thin lacquer-based enamels enough to brush easily, they are so weak in pigment and resin that they are semi-opaque tints, rather than enamels. However, this is a trick worth remembering for special "tinted" wood effects.

For brush application you will probably decide to use one of the synthetic, varnish-based enamels. Follow the finishing procedures for application and rubbing described under the varnish heading, page 41. In brief, it is as follows:

1. Use the varnish tic-tac-toe procedure for applying enamel to a thoroughly repaired and smoothed surface. Apply two or three brush-width-spaced, parallel strokes of enamel. Brush enamel crosswise to fill in the open spaces.

2. Tip off the newly applied enamel surface. Stroke your brush across the strike wire to gently remove any excess paint before tipping off the surface.

3. Work a small enough area for each tic-tac-toe application so that you can complete it and the adjacent area before the first area starts to harden. In tipping off each area, the tipping strokes should cross the dividing line between the older and newer applications. If the older application has started to harden, the leveling effect of the tip-off operation will be lost.

4. Level and scuff sand between coats. Waterproof abrasive paper works as well here.

5. Rub as described for varnish on page 44.

Decorating Techniques

LEAF GILDING on repaired oriental altar is relatively easy (see gilding procedures on pages 54-56).

Glazing

The art of glazing was originally developed to blend color and tone differences in wood surfaces and to make less desirable wood resemble, in color and tones, the more valuable woods. Glazing adds color interest and highlights to carved or flat areas and changes color or tone of the wood surface.

The most common use of the glazing has been in the art of antique imitation. Many beautiful antique reproductions are given the appearance of age by skillful use of glazing. It is quicker to apply a dark glaze over a light finish than wear thin spots through a dark finish.

Glazing is often thought to be applicable only over enamels, but it is used almost as often over clear finishes.

Shading is generally achieved by spraying a pigment or stain-colored lacquer to a feathered-out edge. As shading is one of the more difficult spraying techniques, reference should be made to the spray manufacturer's manual before spraying on a finishing project.

Padding stains are the most useful glazes for use over clear wood finishes to blend color and tone, or to provide a darkened finish normally associated with antiques. Padding-stain forms of glazing provide a more precise control over clear finishes than the pigmented glaze methods.

A pad of lint-free cloth is moistened in padding shellac or lacquer, touched to the dry padding stain powder, then rubbed onto the clear finish. Practice will enable you to produce the desired tone and wood-like color patterning. When thoroughly dry, protect the surface with a compatible varnish or lacquer. Padded glaze is extremely vulnerable without protection.

If you decide to use this process, you will soon find that the standard "padding stain" materials aren't available at most outlets; however, major mail order supply houses in Chicago and New York can provide them.

Antiquing kits contain glazing materials and are available at most paint stores and major paint manufacturers have at least one antiquing kit on the market. Inspection of the kits reveals that most of them are basically a semi-gloss enamel base coat and a thin, pigmented over-glaze which is designed to be partially removed, revealing part of the base coat.

Whether you buy a kit or assemble your own materials, the procedures are essentially the same.

Apply the satin or semigloss enamel as you would for enameling. If the piece is to be "antiqued" by the glazing, a few brushmarks and blemishes won't matter and may help the "aged" look. If, however, you intend to approach the glazing perfection of the French master glazers, you will have to follow all the best enameling techniques with sanding between coats and a final, perfect, velvet smooth coat. Let the piece dry thoroughly.

Brush, pad or spray the glazing material onto the hard, dry enamel surface. You need not be worried about appearance at this stage. Make certain that the coverage is where you want it and that it is complete. Don't cover so large an area that it hardens before you can complete the next step of wiping the surface.

Partial glaze removal is the step that can make or break antique glazing projects. In spite of the instructions supplied with most kits, you should practice wiping techniques beforehand. Different wiping materials and wiping methods produce vastly different results. Try the different effects that can be achieved with coarse burlap, excelsior, cheesecloth, brushes, or plastic wrap.

Brushing across a partially-wiped surface with a stiff-bristled brush, rolled pile carpeting or excelsior will produce a surface having a grained appearance which can look like wood.

Wiping with any material will produce effects which vary with the wiping material's texture and with the completeness of wiping. Hard wiping will remove most of the glaze. Soft wiping with excelsior will produce a streaked effect; with cheesecloth a soft, overall haze can be produced.

Dabbing or stippling with any brush or material can produce a controlled or random pattern, depending on spacing and texture of contact material. A dry brush tip can produce a sandy look; wadded newsprint imparts a pebbly crystalline appearance.

Laying on of stretched or wrinkled material will produce effects including a canvas weave with stretched burlap, a linear random pattern with excelsior, and a marbleized effect with wrinkled plastic wrap.

ANTIQUING KITS

Antiquing kits are available in standard colors, and a few companies have open-stock antiquing materials. Making up your own kit is probably less expensive, and there is the advantage of having customized colors and combinations:

Kits contain any or all of the following:
Semi-gloss or satin enamel or latex base coat
Antiquing glaze
Paint and glaze brushes or pads
Sandpaper
Steel wool
Cheesecloth or burlap

Very few kits have a protective top coat. For the base coat, you can use satin enamel (or glossy enamel or other finish if deglossed with 400 to 600-grit wet-or-dry paper).

Universal pigments, available at a paint store, in a resin sealer or a mixture of satin varnish, boiled linseed oil and turpentine (8:2:1 ratio), will provide an infinite choice of colors for the antiquing glaze.

Color combinations you might try are white with raw umber (in fact, white with almost any color); green with brown, blue, black, or gold; orange with umber; and red with black (Hitchcock chair colors).

A careful look at professionally glazed pieces reveals that glazing was used with restraint. A harsh-edged pattern with too much contrast or too busy a pattern generally produces a novelty item that you may tire of quickly. Glazed pieces offer more artistic freedom than other finishing processes.

If you can't find the antiquing kit you want, make up your own (see box above). Experiment with color combinations. Except for special effects or metallic glaze coats, the brilliant colors are normally used under darker glaze coats to reduce tone and add interest to what might otherwise be too pure a color or too garish an effect. Glazing to tone down the brightness has saved many finishing projects.

Spatter—Random Art

Spatter finishes are intriguing because you can never be quite sure of the result, but if done with taste, they can be extremely beautiful.

Almost any material can be spattered. In fact, many of the modern clear or provincial finishes are slightly spattered to give the fly speck, distressed look.

GLAZES PADDED onto a finished surface provide a wide variety of highlights and accent colors.

SIMULATED WOOD GRAINS are produced by drawing dry brush tip across wet glaze in linear, swirled patterns.

STIPPLED, MOTTLED PATTERNS are made by padding glazed surface with dry sponge or paper towel.

CROSS-HATCH PATTERNS are achieved by pressing piece of burlap or canvas onto wet glaze surface.

MARBLED PATTERNS are made by smoothing clear plastic wrap onto wet glaze surfaces; peel off rapidly.

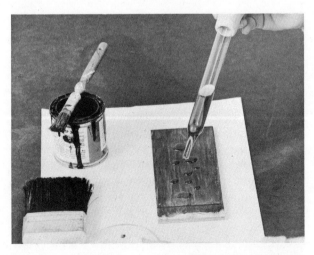

CRATER-LIKE PATTERNS are created by dropping Port wine onto wet glaze; let wine, glaze dry thoroughly.

Where just a few fine specks are to be laid down as in distressing, use a thinned black or very dark version of the base color, in a material that is compatible with the base. Use either a tooth brush or a five-cent metal handled glue or acid brush. Load the brush with the spatter material. The amount of load must be determined by experiment. The wetter the brush the larger the spatter specks. Then draw a finger over the bristles, flicking drops of material off the brush onto the surface. Only practice with a specific type of brush can guide you in aiming the specks.

For larger and more thickly applied spatter spots, experiment with tampico scrub brushes. You may also use artist's hand paint brushes of various sizes to apply the spatter by holding a stick a few inches over the surface and striking the loaded brush sharply down against the stick. For an even more random, larger spot effect, shake a loaded brush over the surface.

Glazes, enamels, lacquers (lacquers on lacquer or shellac surfaces only), latex paints—in fact, just about anything can be used for the spatter. Port wine has been used for antique spotting with standard glazes. You can mix several colors, and an exceptionally interesting effect can be obtained by spattering clear varnish, then gilding the spots with either bronzing powders or leaf, and spattering clear or semi-clear colored glazes over all.

Most spattering, particularly if gilded, should be protected by a top coat of a compatible finish.

Gilding—The Rich Coverup

Earliest uses of gilding included the decoration and enhancement of royal and religious articles. Artifacts found in Egyptian tombs revealed extensive use of gold leaf gilding on wood, resin and plaster surfaces. The techniques for applying the gilding were found to be similar to those used today.

Powder gilding, more properly called bronzing, has taken over from leaf gilding for many items in recent times, because many people believe it is simpler and, in many cases, it is faster than leaf gilding. Powder gilding is less durable, has a less metallic appearance, and dulls more quickly than traditional gilding. In fact, leaf gilding rarely dulls or loses its sheen.

Traditional gilt was seldom applied directly on a smoothed wood surface—the wood was often left rough to provide "tooth" for smoothing materials. The wood surface was covered with plaster of

FLICK BRISTLES of small, stiff brush that has been dipped in thin glaze to make spattered patterns.

STRIKE glaze-coated brush against stick held above surface for larger, irregular spatter designs.

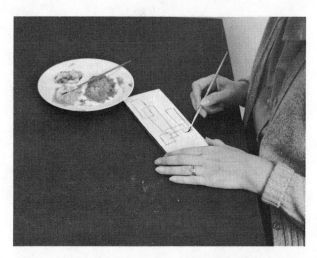

PAINT free-hand patterns or use stencils (see page 63) to produce accents for small areas; apply glaze.

Paris, gesso, burnish gold size, a final size and then with gold leaf. In some instances the plaster or gesso was left out.

Most "carved" gilt frames are actually molded plaster on a flat wooden frame. If you have to repair the carving and if you can duplicate another portion of the same frame, use one of the rubber base molding compounds. It stays flexible, molds with minute detail and can be stored and reused. The "plasticine" molds often recommended are sticky, deform easily and don't store well.

Cast the replacement section in plaster of Paris or one of the filled plastic gels. The plaster is faster, but the plastic is more durable. Fit and glue the cast pieces in place, then fill and shape any gaps using the same materials.

Traditional methods for using bronzing powders and leaf gilt are outlined below. Do not, however, feel that you have to produce a wood texture-free surface with plaster or gesso. Some fine work using leaf gilt on open-grained woods has been produced, so consider all the possibilities, perform some small scale experiments and work for the effect that most pleases you.

Surface preparation for both bronzing and leaf gilding are identical up to the application of the powder or leaf.

If a built-up or carved surface is desired, apply plaster of Paris, shape, dry and smooth with sandpaper and steel wool.

Apply three coats of gesso to sealed-smooth

REMOVE DIRT or loose material from damaged areas on gilded frame before starting repair work.

BUILD UP DAMAGED AREA with spackle or acrylic modeling compound duplicating the remaining carving.

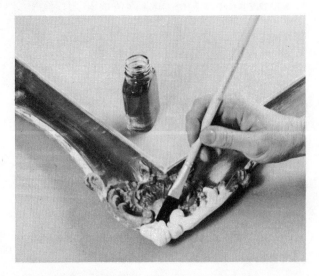

APPLY GESSO to built-up area following directions given above. For bronzing, use varnish based size.

APPLY BRONZE POWDER, then burnish with velvet cloth; protect against hard use with clear finish.

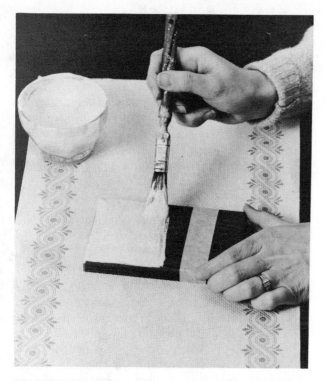

BRUSH GESSO onto surface, let dry, and sand smooth; repeat procedure three times for gilding base.

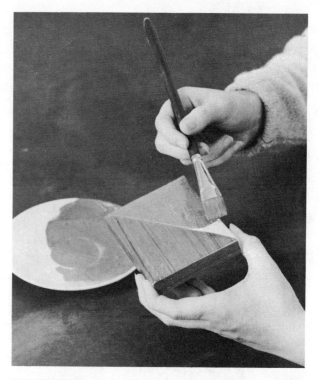

COVER GESSO with gilder's burnish red size or a dull-red acrylic paint to add richness of color.

wood or plaster. Sand as fine and smooth as possible after each coat. Apply and smooth at least three coats of burnish gold size or two of a dull red acrylic color. The burnish gold size permits the finest burnish, but the acrylic colors are easier to obtain. For the ultimate final burnish look, repeat burnish red size two or three more times using 4/0 steel wool as final smoothing on each layer.

Bronzing proceeds by applying a coat of bronzing liquid—a very high grade varnish or slow drying lacquer. The bronzing liquid is permitted to dry to the tacky state—usually 8–24 hours for some varnish bases, 30–60 minutes for the lacquers—before the powder is applied. Test for tackiness by pushing a finger forward across the surface. It should feel tacky but not sticky.

When the bronzing liquid is tacky, lay out a six-inch-square piece of close-piled velvet (black shows gilt powder well), a smaller piece to wrap around your finger tip, some bronzing powder, a few cotton swabs and brushes. A syringe or vacuum cleaner are handy for powder removal.

When the tack is just right, place a small amount of the powder on the square velvet pallet, wrap a finger with the small velvet piece, pile out. Pick up some powder on the velvet finger tip and gently apply it to the tacky surface. Some workers tap it

PICK UP BRONZE POWDER using fingertip covered with velvet; apply to previously sized surface.

GILDER'S RABBIT SKIN SIZE

Rabbit skin glue is available from most art suppliers in granules that look like oversized granules of light brown sugar.

Soak one ounce of the glue in one quart of lukewarm water for half an hour or more, then heat and stir, without boiling, until the glue dissolves. If the glue should start to settle out when it cools, rewarm it and use it warm.

GLUE SIZE must not be heated over 140° F.

on, some brush it on, some roll it on. All methods work. Some workers use all three methods to control the amount of powder applied and its appearance. A fine haze of whiting rubbed onto surrounding areas will reduce unwanted adhesion of bronze or leaf.

Allow the piece to dry for 24 hours; then invert it and tap the back of the piece or use a syringe to gently remove the excess. Overcoating with shellac, varnish or lacquer protects the surface from wear, but metallic sheen is dulled. The use of more than one shade of bronze powder in a random pattern gives an interesting mottled effect.

Gilding-in-the-wind is a name for gilding with leaf gold. The 23-carat leaf gold is less than one quarter of one thousandth of an inch (1/4,000 inch) in thickness.

Having applied the burnish gold size or acrylic artist color and dried them, apply the final size. Here you have a three-way choice—a rabbit skin glue size, a varnish size, or a fast-drying lacquer size. The latter two are available at art stores, and the rabbit skin glue is available at some stores in dry flake form. The varnish and lacquer base sizes are more durable under rough or moist atmosphere handling, but the rabbit skin glue permits burnishing to a superb gleam.

If the varnish or lacquer-based sizes are used, treat them much as you would for bronzing, test for tack, then apply leaf.

Rabbit skin glue size should be applied evenly and allowed to dry to a damp point before the leaf is applied. The exact point of application is difficult to describe but quickly becomes obvious when you experiment with scrap. The size should be just damp enough to hold—not just wet—the leaf. Wet leaf shifts and tears easily.

Leaf application is not very difficult. It is surprisingly forgiving of mistakes. The leaf usually comes in books of 25 four-inch-square leaves with tissue paper dividers. If you decide to cut the leaf for easier handling, cut while holding it between the tissue dividers. Use clean and sharp scissors.

There are several ways of transferring the leaf from tissue to the work surface. Many people simply grasp the leaf and a backup tissue, thumb on tissue and forefinger on leaf; place the lower edge of the leaf with ¼-inch overlap, against the lower edge of the sized area. Then roll the leaf forward onto the surface. Initial contact smoothing is done through the tissue with a cotton ball.

Some craftsmen use a wide, thin, soft, squirrel-hair brush, to make all leaf transfers. They run the brush tip over their hair, then lay it across the leaf. The leaf adheres and can be very neatly transferred without its tissue backing. The tip is used to work the leaf into initial contact with the tacky surface.

The choice of handling leaf is up to the individual. The grasp approach works well, although the finest work appears to come from the practitioners of the tip method.

Lay adjoining leaf so that it overlaps ¼-inch and that all overlaps are in the same direction. Use a soft brush or cotton ball to smooth the leaf into close contact with the tacky size and eliminate all

RUB GOLD LEAF in one direction, being careful not to pick up or damage the overlapped edges.

bubbles of air under the leaf. Patch any voids or breakthrough with scrap leaf. Rub off loose overlapping leaf. Try to work in direction of overlap—not against it, or you will have tear-outs.

Burnish the leaf with an agate burnisher or velvet pad no sooner than eight hours after applying the leaf. Polished agate is obtainable from "rock shops."

If you use the velvet pad, lubricate it very slightly by rubbing a single drop of salad oil into your palm, then draw the pad across the palm.

Should you admire some of the beautifully glazed ivory pieces produced by the French master glazers of Marie Antoinette's day and try to duplicate it by antiquing over an ivory base with raw umber and a touch of bronze, you will probably

GOLD LEAF purchased in looseleaf booklets may often become wrinkled; can be burnished smooth.

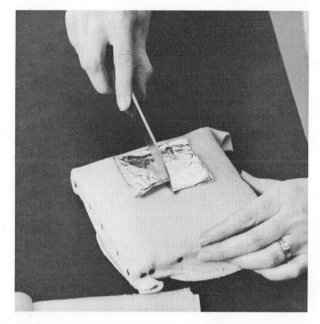

CUTTING of gold leaf is done by drawing sharp knife over leaf placed on chamois-covered pad.

ROLL tissue-backed gold leaf forward onto tacky sized surface, smooth out wrinkles with cotton ball.

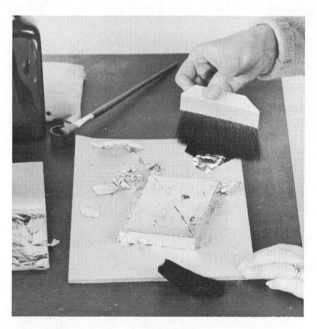

USE GILDER'S TIP (thin, wide brush) as alternate method of transferring gold leaf to surface.

feel cheated, because it won't look just right.

The originals were leaf gilded at the points where gilt highlights were desired, then enameled over in white. At the highlight points the paint was rubbed through to reveal the gold, then glazed with raw umber to obtain the pearlized effect.

Metal leaf in numerous metal and alloy colors are available. They are usually a shade thicker than gold leaf and probably not as durable, but they are more readily available and less expensive.

Bronzing powders in wax and varnish paste formulations, called compos, are now available in cosmetic-type jars or tubes which are extremely useful for quick touchups, or where hard use is not expected. They come in several metallic and pure colors.

Decoupage

Decoupage is said to have started in the late seventeenth century in Italy, and it was popularized in France in the following century. It is one of the most enjoyable arts and one that can be a success with the first try.

Just about anything flat enough to be glued to a surface and finished over is fair game for the decoupager: Pictures, sketches, photographs, cutouts, doilies, fabrics, netting, yarn, metal foils, and confetti. Sources are endless: Magazines, postcards, greeting cards, advertisements, art reproductions, place mats, etc.

Don't feel that you have to accept a given picture as it is. You can cut out the components and

---

EXERCISE IN GILDING, DECOUPAGE, AND GLAZE: DECORATE SOME CANISTERS

You can try your hand at both gilding and decoupage by decorating inexpensive metal canisters with prints and antiqued gold leaf.

In addition to the canisters, you'll need a pint of acrylic gesso; gold size (an adhesive for attaching gold leaf to the gesso); sheets of gold leaf (a bronze imitation; enough to cover 750 square inches costs about $1.50); clear shellac; a tube of raw sienna and one of raw umber acrylic or oil paint (acrylic paints can be thinned with water); pictures or prints; and a can of flat lacquer or mat varnish. You will also need brushes for applying the gesso, shellac, and lacquer, and for pressing on the gold leaf. All these supplies are available at art supply or paint stores.

Apply a coat of unthinned gesso to each canister, following label directions. Gesso sets up in about 20 minutes and is then insoluble.

Next coat the gesso with gold size. Brush the size out to a thin coat; do not go back over the areas you have already covered. Let dry until tacky. There is ample working time from the time the size reaches this stage until it is too dry for the leaf to stick.

Apply the gold leaf to the tacky surface, a sheet at a time, and brush and pat in place. Overlap each sheet about ¼ inch. You can go back and cover up any spots you miss with a dab of size and small pieces of leaf. The leaf will adhere only to the size.

Set the canisters aside to dry for about two days. Then brush off the excess leaf, rub the surface with a soft cloth, and apply a thin coat of clear shellac or lacquer to protect the gold leaf.

When the shellac is dry, you can antique the surface. First apply a glaze of raw sienna and raw umber (see page 49) and wipe it off with a soft cloth almost immediately. Then speckle the surface by dipping an old toothbrush in slightly thinned raw umber glaze and drawing it across a straightedge to spatter the paint.

Once the antiquing is dry, glue the decoupage in place with white glue. As a final step, waterproof the canisters with a coat of mat varnish or flat lacquer.

METAL CANISTERS decorated with magazine prints and gold leaf add color interest to book shelf.

---

rearrange them; you can reverse the whole picture for a reverse image or create a transparent decal-like version of the printed original.

There are two traditional approaches to applying cut-out designs to wood surfaces: Water paste, or glues and varnish sizes. The pastes are resoluble in or, at least, removable with water, and are probably easier to use.

You have the choice of applying the decoupage over clear or enamel finishes. In either case, you should prepare the face before applying the decoupage item.

In brief, the procedure is:

Sand and smooth the surface with at least 6/0 garnet or aluminum oxide paper—finer grit on dense hard wood surfaces under a clear finish.

Apply a sealer appropriate to the top coat; a thinned version of the top coat works well in many cases, or use the product recommended by the top coat manufacturer.

Sand lightly with 6/0 or finer abrasive paper to reduce any irregularities and, in the case of varnishes, to scuff the surface for better adhesion.

Tack rag the surface to clean it of all sanding debris.

Opaque coatings can consist of flat enamel undercoat materials, enamels, latex paints or artist's acrylic paints. The flat undercoats, enamels and paints are available in a multitude of light colors. Dark colors are most often available in the gloss or semi-gloss finishes.

If you use a gloss material, it is a simple matter to wet-sand it with 6/0 or finer wet-or-dry paper to produce a flat or matte surface. You may find it convenient to apply several thinned-down coats, thoroughly wet-sanded and tacked between coats, to produce the best surface to receive the cut-outs.

Be sure to consider your final clear top coat material when selecting the undercoat materials. If you select an undercoat that softens and lifts under a specific top coat, you will waste time and effort.

Good combinations are enamels and enamel undercoaters under varnishes; and latex, pigmented vinyl stains and artist's acrylics under lacquers. When using lacquer, spray a couple of fine mist coats before heavier build-up coats to prevent colors from print or base material from being dissolved and worked into the top coat.

If you decide to use the varnish size method of gluing the material, apply a smooth coating of the selected size (gliders' oil size or varnish). Allow it to dry until it is no longer liquid but still tacky.

Carefully lay the cut-out on the tacky surface and burnish it down with a smooth metal, bone

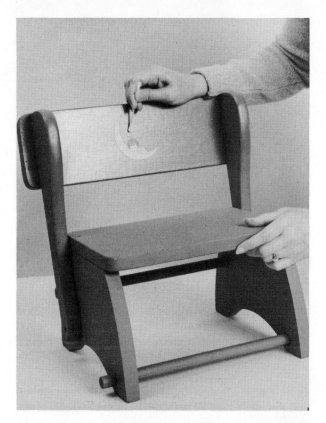

DECOUPAGED CUT-OUTS made from greeting cards, make lively decorations for children's furniture.

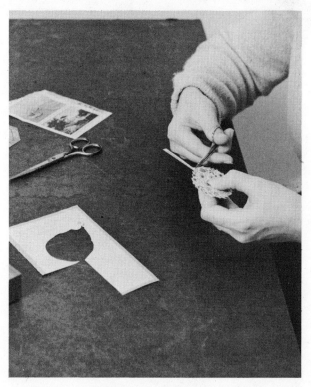

USE SMALL SCISSORS (straight and curved) to trim intricate parts of cut-out; crisp edges are essential.

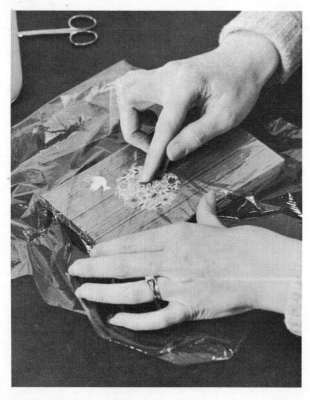

THIN PAPER CUT-OUTS can often show print from reverse side when moistened with glue; handle carefully.

or hardwood burnishing stick. WARNING: Once it's down on the tacky surface, it probably can't be successfully moved, so be sure of location before contacting.

Gluing or pasting the material down gives you a little more leeway for error, since you can move the cut-out after it contacts the surface, and clean-up is easier.

The problem with water-based pastes and glues is that they tend to wet paper, causing it to wrinkle and become more transparent, which is a problem if there is printing on the back side of the cut-out. To lessen this possibility, use one of the very fast drying spray-can, clear lacquers, or artist's fixatives. Apply the spray as a fine mist—do *not* wet or drench the surface. Allow the first application to dry, then repeat two or three more times to shield the paper to reduce wetting and wrinkling.

If there is a possibility that the printing on the back of a cut-out will show through when mounted, abandon the traditional methods and proceed to the use of polymer artist's medium described below.

Place the cut-out face down on a clean, smooth surface. Wax paper is good provided that none of the wax gets pressed into the surface of the material to be decoupaged. Wax can interfere with sub-

PLACE GLUED CUT-OUT on surface and cover with clear plastic wrap; use fingertip to rub out wrinkles.

SPRAY OR BRUSH numerous layers of clear finish over cut-out until it looks buried in the surface.

sequent top coats. Coat the back of the material with paste or glue. Be sure to have a complete coat —any voids show up as bubbles later. To subdue the wrinkling effect of water base material on paper, try a "non-wrinkling" paste, an acrylic polymer artist's medium, or, at least, use the heaviest bodied brand of white glue.

Place one edge of the glued material in contact with the prepared surface, then roll it forward, making continuous contact to eliminate air bubbles. Lay a piece of plastic sheeting over the design, and roll the surface to ensure firm contact.

Remove plastic cover and excess glue. A damp rag works well for removing most glues. Allow the glue to dry thoroughly.

Finish the project with the top coat appropriate to the undercoat and glue stages. Use varnish over a gilder's oil or varnish size, and either varnish or lacquer over the glue size. The differences between varnish and lacquer for decoupage are the fast drying and multicoating characteristics of lacquer versus the much slower drying and multicoating of varnish. However, varnish can build up a thick finish with fewer coats than lacquer, possibly offsetting some of lacquer's speed of drying.

Apply the finish as generously as possible without encouraging sags, puddles, runs, etc. Allow the film ample time to dry—at least twice the maximum time recommended by the manufacturer.

Level sand between each coat, and continue applications until the lip or outline of the design can no longer be detected through the finish.

The final coat should be rubbed down to remove any minor imperfections and to produce a soft eggshell or satin glow. Waterproof silicon carbide papers in 400 to 600-grits can be used for final wet rubs. You can also use pumice and rottenstone in oil or water lubricants as described on page 38.

Modern techniques and materials add some interesting variations to decoupage. Artist's acrylic varnishes and gels allow you to achieve transparent, decal-like designs on opaque or transparent materials and to achieve a reverse image of the original. Artists' supply outlets carry acrylic polymer gloss medium and varnish. The acrylic medium is a chalk-white fluid with the consistency of varnish, which can be cleaned with water.

A word of warning—if you intend to produce a reverse transfer, make sure that you remove or block out any lettering with printers ink. It will show up as reversed or "mirror" lettering if you don't.

DECOUPAGE PLAQUES are good projects for beginners; obtain materials in ready-made kits at art stores.

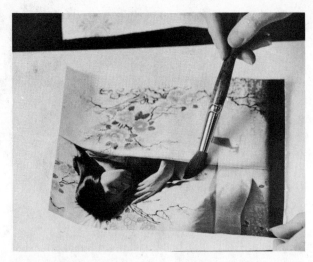

COVER DESIGN with a thin coating of acrylic varnish; when it has dried thoroughly, apply second coat.

PLACE VARNISHED DESIGN face down in a detergent solution until the paper backing is ready to remove.

SMOOTH-OUT CURLED EDGES of finished decal before placing onto wet surface of acrylic varnish.

A reverse transfer is made by coating both the prepared surface and the FACE of the print to be transferred. Allow both to dry thoroughly. Heat from an infra-red bulb or the lowest possible heat in an oven with a trustworthy control (leaving the door slightly open helps keep the temperature low) can speed drying. If you air dry, allow 24 hours; if you heat dry, wait until the heated surface loses tack, then cool and air dry for an hour.

Apply a second coat to surface and print face. Allow it to set for about 5 minutes until it loses its liquid look but has ample tackiness. Then apply the print face down on the surface. Smooth out all bubbles immediately.

Repeat the drying procedure used previously but for safety allow an additional 24 hours air drying time before proceeding.

Remove the paper from the print by wetting the paper backing and rubbing gently until it peels free of the plastic face.

For a fast and complete soaking of the paper, add a wetting agent to the water, a photographer's wetting agent, 1 part vinegar to 1 part water, or enough liquid detergent to produce a soapy feeling. If you use shellac as a clear undercoat surface, use the acid, vinegar-water version, or you will mar the shellac surface.

Rub the center area of the paper backing until the fibers roll up, then work toward the edges until all traces of paper are removed. You will find the ink has remained on the plastic film surface. Dry the surface thoroughly, at least 12 hours, then apply a level coat of the acrylic polymer varnish.

Level sand the dry surface, and build up the finish with more coats of the polymer varnish or gel, varnish or lacquer, as desired. Level sand between coats and give a final rub to the top coat.

If you have decoupaged on a plaque or other surface where an artist's brush stroked surface is desired, use the polymer gel for textured effects. When you first apply it, you will lose sight of the surface under the chalky white gel coat. Brush or texture it with spatula, sponge, fingers or comb; watch the surface come through as the gel dries and becomes transparent. Several products are available which provide surface age or cracking.

Decal-like transparencies can be made from printed material by simply coating the face of the print with the polymer gloss varnish, drying it, recoating, then drying it again. When thoroughly dry, soak it in a pan of soapy water and rub the paper backing until it is completely removed from the plastic film formed by the acrylic varnish. When dry, the

FOR DECOUPAGE IDEAS...TRY PHOTOGRAPHY

Don't overlook photography as a source for decoupage. Your camera can provide enlarged or reduced black and white (color tends to fade rapidly) duplicates of items otherwise unavailable, either because they are the wrong size, or because they are part of a valuable book or collection.

Keep in mind that decoupage is a copyist art —other people's originals are used in new and interesting ways. Don't be afraid to copy all or part of anything as long as it is not specifically forbidden by law (United States stamps, money, etc.,) or does not infringe on someone else's property rights.

Negative and positive photostats, black and white prints, toned or tinted prints, colored prints from engineering reproduction papers, and blueprints are just a few of the many possibilities to consider for use. The three projects shown in the photographs here could easily be converted by photographic means for use as decoupage.

Photograms (shown in top photo) are simply silhouettes of natural or manmade objects which are made by placing the objects in direct contact with the face of photographic enlarging paper, and then exposing it to a strong light.

The exposure to light can be extended from 10 to 30 minutes (depending on paper used) until the paper visibly darkens. It should then be fixed in photographers' hypo solution, washed, then dried. If short light exposures under darkroom conditions are used, follow the standard processing methods which are detailed in the instruction sheets accompanying most photographic printing paper.

Stamps from many countries of the world (shown in middle photo) are exquisite works of art and often look as good or better than the original when reproduced as monochrome enlargements for decoupage. Since the originals are small, be sure to use the finest grain film and developer combination, and the largest negative size available. Fill as much of the negative with the image as possible.

Rubbings (shown in bottom photo) of tombstones, historical markers, or cornerstones make wonderful decorative accents. Reduced or enlarged photographically, they can fit any project at hand. Miniatures of rubbings from manhole covers make marvelous medallions for "Oriental" furniture and jewelry.

In addition to the projects discussed above, other items available to the decoupage enthusiast with a camera are lithographs, wood cuts, Oriental scrolls, tapestries, stitcheries, mosaics, sculpture, animal tracks in sand, silhouettes, Christmas ornaments, stained glass, and origami.

PHOTOGRAMS made with artificial light and developer are black and white with various tones of gray.

ENLARGED STAMPS mounted on boxes, trays, or bookends can be used for gifts or kept for display.

RUBBINGS made with colored wax or crayons can be photographically reduced, used as decoupage accents.

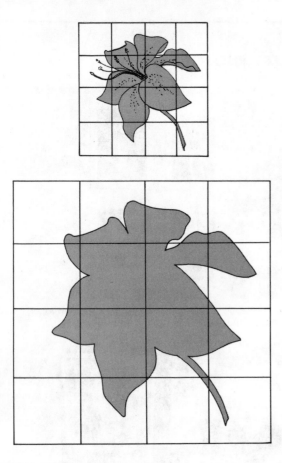

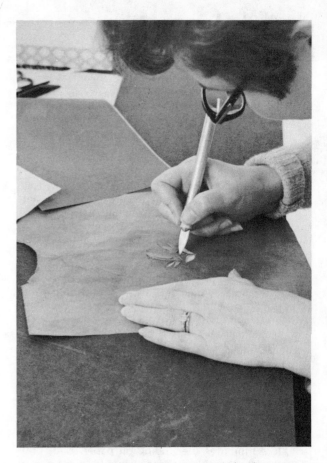

DRAW GRID over original design; make enlarged grid to redraw actual-sized pattern on stencil paper.

CUT OUT DESIGN with a sharp craft knife or razor blade, place on surface, and carefully apply paint.

plastic film will show a somewhat foggy transparency of the original print. The fogginess is the imprint of the texture of the missing paper and will vanish when glued.

The transparency can now be cut out and glued to a prepared surface with either polymer varnish or white glue.

If you plan to apply it to a natural wood or to a painted surface, and a quick check shows that the color or grain interferes with the design, coat the back of the transparency with a thin coat of polymer gloss varnish pigmented with artist's acrylic paints approximately the color of the original paper backing. Dry the pigmented coating thoroughly before gluing the decal.

An amusing variation, especially for children's furniture, is to distort the image on the transparency, prior to gluing it down. Dip it in hot water, stretch it, then hold the stretched shape until it cools. Glue it down with either polymer varnish or glue. The transparent decals may be top coated and treated as other decoupage projects.

Stenciling

Stenciled designs are a convenient way to create the floral patterns or arabesques often associated with provincial or peasant pieces of furniture. In America, stenciling is usually associated with Hitchcock chairs or Pennsylvania Dutch pieces.

You may decide to paint designs using artist's oil colors in a varnish medium (2 parts varnish to 1 part distilled turpentine) and applied with water color brushes or Oriental bamboo brushes.

Examine some decorated pieces and notice the colors, shapes and relative size and positioning. Make use of the several books on peasant, vegetable, heraldic and geometric design ideas. These books can show you ways to conventionalize or simplify otherwise complex shapes and designs.

Either obtain a book on stencil making or purchase several ready-made stencils at an art supply store, and study the manner in which they are made. You will notice that there are "ties" connecting adjoining parts. In the more complex de-

USE FINE BRUSH to bring out details and provide visual contrast to design; apply finish if desired.

SPRAY PAINT can also be used to make stencils; cover object with wax paper to prevent overspray.

signs, the placing of the ties becomes quite an art and is best learned by observation and experience. The ties should be inconspicuously and logically worked into the design.

Use a stiff stencil paper sold at art and paint stores or make your own by saturating heavy brown *kraft* wrapping paper on both sides with boiled linseed oil or shellac (use the one least likely to be affected by the paints, varnishes or lacquers you will be using) and hanging it up to dry. *Mylar,* a tough sheet plastic available at drafting supply houses, works well and is transparent.

Whether your design is from nature, illustration or an original work, you will have to make a drawing or tracing to the final size you intend to use. You can use the graph paper approach or ask a photographer friend or local processor to enlarge or reduce the design to the desired size. It is a fairly easy operation for any competent photographer, provided you give him a good original. Trace only the essential outlines—don't try to include detail—to suggest the subject.

Transfer your drawing to the stencil paper by means of dressmaker's tracing or carbon paper. Lay the marked stencil over 8 or 10 sheets of newsprint, place thumb tacks at the corners, then carefully cut out those portions to be removed. Shading-in sections to be removed helps to prevent mistakes. A very sharp, single-edged razor blade, or the scalpel-like blade of a knife with replaceable blades prevents ragged edges.

Rather than have one complicated stencil for groupings of flowers or fruit, many workers make separate stencils for each. This method gives a greater freedom in composition to fit specific furniture pieces and ensures slight handmade differences even when duplicating.

A neutral background is probably best because it enhances the richness of the stencil. A neutral, dark, matte background is ideal. Whichever the color you choose, experiment in neutralizing the strong pure color by adding a touch of its complementary color, browns or black so that the raw color doesn't overpower the stenciling.

Apply the matte ground color in the area to be stenciled; allow it to dry thoroughly for at least 48 hours.

Paint stenciling, either color or metallic pigments, calls for taping the stencil into close contact with the surface, then applying the desired paints with a stencil brush. Brushes designed for stenciling resemble shaving brushes. Load the bristles with paint, tap on newsprint to remove excess, then apply to stencil.

Always work from the stencil to the open areas, and move the brush in a direction natural to the subject. That is, brush in the direction of ribbing on leaves and texture or reflections. Actual veining, repairing or detailing can be done by hand with a fine sable or bamboo brush. When dry, the stenciling can be glazed or shaded with bronzing powders.

Bronze powder stenciling begins with a coat of varnish size over a neutral background previously laid down. When the size is tacky, press the stencil into place—a gentle finger rub around the cut openings will make the edges tack to the surface and ensure a crisp edge. Then using the velvet palette and velvet wrapped finger tip, described on page 53, apply the bronze powders.

Be sure to remove excess powder from the velvet finger tip. Excess bronze leaves a fluffy unattached surplus in the cut-outs that scatters over the background when the stencil is removed. If you should apply too much to an area, try lifting it off with cotton, or by vacuuming.

Don't brush toward the stencil; it will collect at the edge and work its way under the stencil to smear a crisp edge. If any unwanted powder reaches the neutral background, remove it when dry with 4/0 steel wool on a finger tip or wrapped around a cotton swab.

Work from the stencil to the center of the open area with either a circular motion or one which parallels an important texture or highlight. Varying the pressure varies the density of deposit, so let up where a shaded effect is desired. Remember, although there are many metal colors, shades and pure colors available in bronzing powders, you can obtain interesting effects by applying transparent colored or antiquing glazes over gold and silver bronzed stencils.

Glazes over stencils are easily applied by first coating the bronzed or painted stencil work with a shellac coat and then using an oil glaze over it.

If the glaze is not pleasing, a little turpentine removes it but leaves the shellac-protected stencil intact. For pigmented color glazes, any of the oil base glazes used in normal glazing or oil paints may be used. For metallic gold, silver or copper, mix sufficient bronzing powders with a varnish glaze base until a thick paste is produced (metallic compos, as they are known, are available commercially in tubes and cosmetic-type jars).

Your finger tips are the finest tools for applying glazes and highlights to the dry stencil. Use the tip of either your index or middle finger, to pick up tiny amounts of the glaze or compo and apply them with a light touch to the stencil. Spread them out, rub and texture them. Add more material, remove excess or blend with an adjoining finger. Finish by buffing lightly with a soft lintfree cloth stretched tightly over a finger. Use a gentle rocking motion and buff with the fleshy edge of the palm.

For maximum durability, the design should be protected by shellac, varnish or lacquer. If you use varnish and expect to renew the clear finish in the future, put a shellac coat between the stenciled design and the varnish coat.

Leaf gild stenciling was often used on quality furniture of the Hitchcock and Empire periods, but it is difficult for most home craftsmen. The steps are exactly the same as for bronze powder stenciling, except that leaf is layed over the stencil and forced into the open spaces with a piece of plush or plush-like carpet. It is then burnished through the stencil.

Striping

Although really intricate spider webbing is difficult without practice, simple edge lining, the major striping used on furniture, is fairly simple. People tend to forget a basic trick they probably used in kindergarten, as soon as they try to use a brush to draw a straight line. Do you remember drawing a straight margin line down one side of a pad of paper by starting at the top, placing your third and little fingers on the edge of the pad, and drawing the pencil toward you? The same trick works for striping. The only difference is that you use a brush and hold it semi-horizontally instead of vertically as with the pencil.

Other tips on striping are: 1) Thoroughly remove grease and wax from the surface with mineral spirits or denatured alcohol (no alcohol if the base is shellac or a sensitive lacquer); 2) Use a good varnish based enamel (or varnish based size if gild-

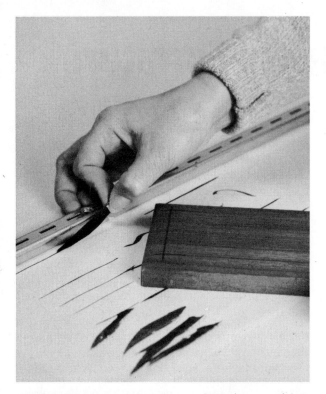

STRIPING is done with a dagger-shaped, squirrel hair brush; fine and uniform lines are required.

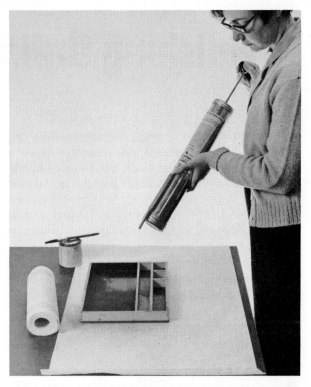

FLOCKING with a hand sprayer is remarkably easy and inexpensive; oversprayed fibers can be reused.

ing) which, for good flow, may be thinned with one part turpentine or recommended thinner, to eight parts enamel or varnish (1:8); 3) Lay down a shield coat of shellac on the base coat surface prior to striping so that any enamel or varnish striping errors can be simply wiped off with mineral spirits.

Arrange your finger guides. Use an edge of the project, straight edge, draftsman's French curve, or a piece of ⅛ or ¼-inch pressboard cut to shape and held in place with pressure-sensitive tape.

Dip the striping brush all the way to the heel, just below the metal ferrule, and draw it across the strike wire on the paint can—lacking a strike wire, you can use the lip of the can. Make a practice stroke or two until the enamel flows well without spreading or bulging the stripe. The practice strokes usually remove ¼ to ½ of the paint load of the brush. Use the remainder to lay down the stripe by using the finger guide and drawing the brush toward you in a continuous motion.

Flocking

Flocking is the art of adhering thousands of small fibers together to give the appearance of felt. Most art and craft supply stores have flocking kits and materials.

Flocking provides a soft touch to specialty finishing projects such as inner sections of picture frames, stenciled patterns, and as protective linings for drawers and boxes.

First seal any porous surface to be flocked. Apply a colored undercoat or size and "blow" the flocking fibers onto the freshly applied size. Allow the surface to dry 12 to 24 hours. Shake and brush to remove excess fibers.

The simplest flock blower is identical to those sold at nurseries for applying agricultural insecticide dusts. Unless you are working on a large project, there is no need to use a power flock sprayer.

The flock fibers are available in wool, silk, cotton, rayon, and other materials. Rayon is the one most available and is adequate for most projects. Fibers are available in a range of 26 colors, each with a matching undercoat or size. The undercoat can be replaced by good quality and slightly thinned-down enamels and varnishes. But until you have experimented, use the manufacturer's undercoat. You can apply the undercoat through stencils by brush or sprayer, then flock to produce patterns on frames, mirrors, gift paper, and wall paper.

Finishing Unfinished Furniture

Unfinished furniture is often considered for those situations where intended use or budget rule out more expensive finished furniture. There is a wide variation in the quality and price of the unfinished furniture available. Some finely built pieces in classic and modern designs and fine cabinet woods are available and should be treated to the finest finishes that can be put on them. Some exceedingly fine reproductions of Early American pine pieces are available and should not be confused with other pine furniture that is so readily obtainable.

Preparations

Fine unfinished furniture should be prepared and finished by the procedures detailed throughout this book. Examine the piece carefully to determine whether any repairs must be made to the surfaces or joints. While generally well made, the furniture may have been damaged during delivery.

Inexpensive mass produced unfinished furniture is often nailed together and often built of mismatched lumber—seldom cabinet grade wood.

WALNUT CABINET was finished with fine penetrating resin. For glossier finishes, use lacquer or varnish.

Check all joints and drawers, especially on case goods (chests, dressers, etc.), since the nailing often looks tight but when the wood shrinks slightly, the nails tend to loosen.

Disassemble joints and re-glue, if necessary. Many times on case goods it is possible to use a thin blade to spread a loosely nailed joint. Add glue, re-nail, or clamp. If the joint won't spread and needs glue, try rocking the joint, forcing the glue into the opening and closing the gap. Should that fail, use a glue injector as described on page 17.

Repair obvious defects and round off all knife-sharp edges. Sharp edges may look good when new, but they soon shed finishes and wear through.

For aging, use a wood rasp, abrasive paper, or knife to reproduce the effects of wear. Antique imitators make liberal use of rasps, abrasives, rough edged grinding wheels rolled across a surface to produce scars, chains of keys to produce nicks and gouges; and small drills or charges of bird shot to produce worm holes.

Applying the Finish

Generally, the best approach is to enamel, following the procedures given on page 47. The degree of perfection will depend on your own desires and the use to which you intend to put the furniture.

Don't forget antiquing, glazing, gilding or decoupage as possible disguises for an inexpensive piece—it's amazing what a good cosmetic job does for an otherwise uninspired table or chest of drawers.

If you want some semblance of wood finish, but the surface has much to hide, use a pigmented wiping type stain. Some relatively new liquid and foam wiping stain products with a vinyl base make the job quite easy. Besides the ten wood colors currently available, you can obtain the water-clear version and mix your own colors with tubes of universal tinting colorants available at most paint stores. Be creative. Orange stripes on brown—or any combination—are possible, since colors can go on top of each other without smear and they can be blended.

If the job is fairly small, you might consider using spray varnish or lacquer. As long as you are using spray, you might as well take advantage of fast drying of lacquer.

Standard woodworker's transparent stains work well and are worth using if you are fortunate to find an inexpensive piece with matched boards. Even mismatched boards can be salvaged by blending with pigmented vinyl or oil stains.

Colorful effects can be obtained by use of common fabric dyes (dark brown, for example, resembles walnut) enamels, lacquers, or tinting colors in virtually any finishing vehicle you can name (thinned varnish, shellac, lacquer, etc.).

Milk paint creates an interesting finish, and is easy to make. Mix powdered skim milk with water to the consistency of a heavy bodied flat wall paint. Add dry or universal colorants to achieve the color you want. Mix it initially in small one-half to one-cup batches. If you intend to duplicate the colors of older pieces, add a touch of the complementary color, brown or black to neutralize the clear colors of the tints. Apply it as you would flat wall paint. It should dry flat in about an hour; allow three or more days to harden before using. A steel wool rub and waxing will brighten the surface.

Working With Fir

Fir and fir plywood are not too often used in unfinished furniture, except for backs of cabinets or drawers. However, it is frequently used for built-in cabinets and shows up enough in unfinished pieces to warrant special note.

As with many fast growing conifers, it has a wild grain. That is, the grain differs in absorption between the summer and winter wood of each growth ring. Liquids are absorbed quickly in the softer areas and remain on the surface at the hard portions to cause erratic grain color differences. Most of your effort will be in subduing the grain and smoothing the surface.

Wild grain can be greatly controlled by use of any of the several fir-ply sealers on the market in both clear and white pigmented forms. The wipe-on, wipe-off white versions have a tendency to lighten the softwood and leave the harder wood unchanged. This counterbalances the absorption of any dark stain in the soft areas by providing a partial barrier and a light base.

A plus factor with the grain sealers is that they also seal the surface against moisture to prevent

BENT NAILS in drawer assembly indicate poor workmanship; disassemble and reglue before finishing.

checking on fir plywood. The grain sealer must be thoroughly soaked into the surface, including the edges. Penetrating resin floor and furniture finishes also work well. Avoid shellac-based grain sealers; they do not seal against moisture effectively.

Sanding fir and fir plywood can be a problem. Unsealed surfaces have such wide variations in hardness between the summer and winter wood of the growth rings that the harder portions sand slowly, and the softer portions sand poorly and too fast. The result can be a wavy, dip and hollow effect with a good surface on the harder and naturally darker portions and a poor surface in between.

A sanding sealer or preferably a first coat of one of the commercial fir-ply sealers will handle the softwood problem by hardening the softer wood fibers enough for fine sanding. A sanding block large enough to bridge the largest softwood area will prevent a wavy, hollowed-out surface.

Grain sealing techniques are equally important for clear or enamel finishes. Don't fail to use a commercial fir-ply sealer. Enamel undercoats and thinned enamel work well as first coats on hardwoods but not on most woods of the fast growing conifer or soft-wood group.

Staining fir and fir plywood that has been sealed and sanded is fairly trouble-free, providing all of the sealer hasn't been removed by the sanding from the softwood areas. Staining on unsealed fir will result in a greatly accentuated grain pattern, with the soft areas taking most of the stain and coming out considerably darker.

Wiping stains, particularly the water-based vinyl emulsions, are a natural for fir, since they tend to mask much of the undesirable wild grain.

If problems with sap streaking or resinous knots should occur, refer to the pine section below.

Working With Pine

Pine is probably the single most widely used wood for unfinished furniture, and it has several of the same disadvantages as fir, plus a few more. The wild grain, the soft and hard portions of the annual rings, and the sealing should be handled exactly as for fir. The problems peculiar to pine are knots, sap pockets, and streaks. The presence of sap is usually part of a knot problem.

Sapstreaks and pockets are best handled by scraping away prominent surface deposits with as little damage to the wood as possible. Then, use turpentine or mineral spirits to soften and remove as much of the remainder as possible. A little hard rubbing may be called for as well as several reapplications of turpentine. When the treated surfaces dry, stain the surface if staining is required, then coat only the immediate area around the sap deposits with a wash coat of 1 to 1½-pound cut shellac, unless you intend using shellac as a surface sealer, in which case, coat the entire surface. The shellac will shield the top coats from the sap. Remember that some finishes won't take shellac undercoats, so be selective in your choice of top-coat material.

Knots should be treated like sapstreaks with a solvent wash, staining if required, shellac shielding, and topcoat. Knots may also require some filling in.

Fast Finishes

Many finishers of unfinished furniture are looking for attractive finishes requiring minimum work in application and upkeep, and don't feel the need to follow fine finishing methods on the furniture they consider temporary. In fact, it would seem to be a waste of time and effort to go through the ultimate varnish procedures for an unfinished fir chest intended for temporary use, unless it is, in effect, a practice piece for varnishing a fine piece later on.

A brief rundown of the quick but attractive finishes follows below. Remember, however, that any attractive finish must be preceded by good surface preparation.

Tinting with thinned-down, colored enamels, lacquers, or colored fir-ply sealers is probably the simplest one-step finishing method.

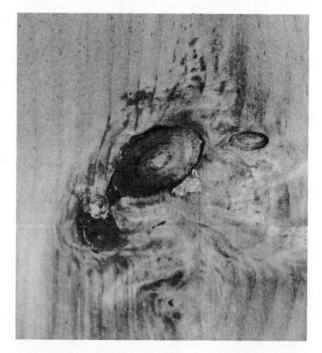

KNOTS often hide sap pockets; must be thoroughly cleaned with solvent, then sealed with shellac.

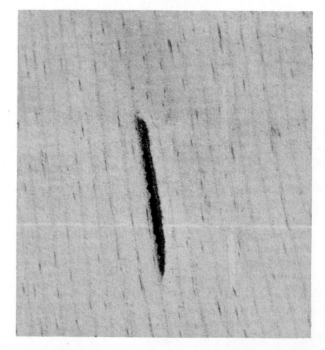

SAP STREAKS are sticky or dry gashes in the grain; must be carefully cleaned and shellac sealed.

Simply add tinting colors to standard fir-ply sealer and apply as directed or thin down standard enamels or colored lacquers — depending upon consistency, color, and effect desired. Use from full-strength to half thinner and half original material. Apply by brushing or padding on, then wipe off much as you would a glaze. On some of the wild grain soft woods, you may want to use a shellac wash coat to prevent absorption of the tinting material into the surface. A tinted surface may be clear top-coated for durability with any compatible lacquer or varnish finish.

The simplest of all clear finishes, and probably the most repairable, is the penetrating resin finish (see page 35). It works best over penetrating stains (water, N.G.R., oil) but can be used over pigmented oil stains — providing the stain has no sealer component such as varnish or vinyl. Almost as simple is the penetrating resin finish with a floor varnish additive described on page 35.

Hard paste wax might seem to be the simplest of all finishes to put over a raw, stained, or filled wood surface. But, when you think of the inevitable necessity of buffing and surface repair, it ranks second to the penetrating resin finishes that harden and seal the surface.

Latex house and wall paints and enamels can provide a fast and colorful finish for unfinished furniture and are available in a variety of colors to match, blend, and harmonize with walls, drapes, furnishings and other surroundings. Interesting use can be made of the same paint used for the wall against which the finished piece will stand. Experiment with tinting the original paint to emphasize one of its color components, or to neutralize it with additions of its color complement. If the wall paint cannot withstand chest or table top usage, top-coat it with clear lacquer. Most clear finishes will add color — usually yellow — to a painted surface. This is most obvious on light surfaces.

Glazes, whether antiqued, wiped, grained, marbled, spattered, or mottled, are the easiest finishes to apply for quick decoration. Such finishes are most easily applied in the form of a latex undercoat and an oil or varnish based glaze (see page 49). If varnish-based base coats are used, apply a shellac shield coat between the base coat and the oil or varnish glaze. Coat the glazed surfaces with a compatible spray lacquer or varnish. Be sure to apply a light first spray coat of the clear top coat on

thoroughly dry (24 hrs.) glaze. Dry the first coat at least 24 hours before recoating.

Enamel, varnish, and lacquer, in that order, are increasingly difficult to apply, although lacquer is the easiest if good spray equipment is available. You can save time on rubdown where eggshell, semi-gloss, or matte surfaces are desired by using an appropriate non-gloss product for the topmost coat.

Decoupage can be also used to cover mismatched materials with restrained or challenging effects, as you choose. Remember that on a piece of furniture that is not scrutinized closely, decoupage materials need not be as thoroughly buried in the top coats as in traditional decoupage. In fact, a crisp-edged collage effect can be extremely attractive.

Char and brush is one finishing method that looks good on redwood, pine, fir, and cedar — especially on random-grained rather than pin-stripe grained surfaces.

Simply use a propane torch with a flame spreader to burn the surface enough so that the soft wood portion of the grain is charred, leaving the harder wood sections relatively unscathed. A little practice will show that you can keep the flame moving slowly over the surface just ahead of the slightly yellowish surface flames of the burning softwood. The wood supported flames will usually die out as the torch flame passes. A quick wipe with a moist (not wet) rag will subdue any others.

Use a stiff wire brush to brush out the charred soft-wood parallel to the grain. You can control the color of the finished product by the amount and force of brushing. The wood tones that brush through the black are in shades of gold through brown and red.

Finish the surface with a paste wax or a penetrating resin to prevent the charred wood from rubbing off and staining.

Opportunities for experimentation are provided by unfinished furniture. Be adventuresome and try some of the newer finishing products that appear from time to time. Use them exactly as directed before trying any short-cuts — too many fine products have been dismissed as useless simply because directions were not followed.

Look for manufacturer's literature on specific products, finishing systems, and hobby applications. Much effort is spent in promotion by manufacturers and the resulting literature often serves as a good general guide and as a source of ideas.

Repairing a Faulty Finish

Many a beautiful piece of furniture with a shoddy-looking finish has been revived with cleaning and finish restoration. Before attempting any finish repair, determine whether the finish is shellac, lacquer, or varnish. Cleaning with household ammonia in water may work well on lacquer or varnish, but it will dissolve shellac. (Use the chart on page 6 to determine the type of finish.) Remember, anything made before 1850 that still has its original finish is probably finished in shellac; anything made after 1850 and before 1920 probably has a modified shellac finish requiring alcohol-lacquer thinner combinations of 1:1 or 2:1 for solvent. A piece finished after 1920 probably has a lacquer finish. A very few custom made or refinished items may have varnish or built-up hard oil finishes.

Defects and Their Repair

Blushing is a white overall surface haze similar to a white spot, although it is less severe. The cure is to wear away a fraction of the frosted surface to reach a clear level. Use a mild abrasive: Rottenstone and water or rubbing oil, 3/0 or 4/0 steel wool and rubbing oil, or pumice and water or rubbing oil. Always use a felt pad or felt-padded block when using rottenstone or pumice. Rottenstone is the mildest and safest abrasive, pumice is the fastest cutting and easiest to overcut with—so go slow with pumice.

Chipping is usually the result of a blow that removes a flake of finish. The cure is to fill, level, and finish the chip. Methods include shellac and wax stick filling, liquid shellac, lacquer, varnish, or enamel buildup.

The liquid buildups are accomplished by leveling with as many layers as necessary. They are applied by a fine, soft, artist's brush. Wet the edges of the chip, but remove any overlap, and dry each layer thoroughly. Drying time depends on the material: minutes for lacquer, an hour or two for shellac, and a day or two for varnish. Use abrasive paper, on a hard rubber or wooden block, with rubbing oil to reduce excess buildup. A large block, 4 × 5-inches, provides enough surface to prevent edge or corner gouging.

When the repair area is sanded flat, wash the surface with 1:1 vinegar and water solution; dry. If necessary, a pumice or rottenstone and oil rub will more nearly match it to surrounding areas.

Wax sticks can be used to fill very small chips. The traditional method is the use of melted shellac stick as explained on page 72.

Cigarette burns should be scraped clear of burn debris, then filled with shellac-stick or wax stick (see page 72). If the wood still looks burnt, a glaze of a lighter wood tone will often hide the black.

Cracking and crazing is caused by expansion and contraction of the wood forcing the less flexible finish film to part in a pattern of lines. It is called "crazing" if the lines are fine and "cracks" if they are large. The condition results from moisture or heat. Also, direct sunlight may have bleached the wood or stain. If the color is good, and the finish is shellac or lacquer, you can reamalgamate the finish by using the appropriate solvent (see pages

REPAIR DENTS by using bottle cap between hot iron and moist pad; steam will swell and raise dent.

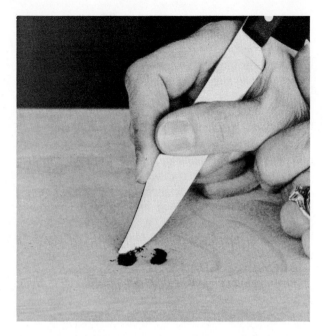

SCRAPE AREA of cigarette burns removing charred and loose material before proceeding with repairs.

GENERAL CLEANING with solvents or soap and water can remove dirt and mars on built-up waxes.

71-72). If it is varnish, you MIGHT build up with a 1:1 turpentine-boiled linseed oil mixture, but it is generally best to strip the piece and start over.

Crumbling, powdered, or flaked finishes may be treated as cracked and crazed finishes. The finish should be stripped and refinished.

Dents, dings, and pressure marks can be worked out by filling the wood cells around the dent with water. The moisture expands the compressed cells back to normal. On bare wood, simply apply a hot, wet pad or press a wet pad over the dent with an iron or soldering iron tip. It may take several treatments. When the surface is finished, remove the local finish and patch later. Or, you might use a sharp pushpin or needle to make holes in the wood to allow entry of water and steam. Refinish any remaining depression with a shellac stick or the original finish.

Inlay damages are fairly easy to repair. If you have the original inlay piece, remove the old glue, then reglue the piece in place.

If the inlay piece is missing, clean and even out any jagged edges. Take a piece of matching veneer from a less conspicuous spot and glue it in place. Use the thinnest and sharpest edges possible when cutting veneer. Cut it slightly oversize at first, because it's easier to cut away than to add wood. Finish it to match the surface before cutting. If veneer is unavailable, clean and stain the hole somewhat lighter than the missing veneer, then fill with transparent shellac stick.

Lacquer finish reamalgamation is accomplished by brushing or padding lacquer thinner on the damaged lacquer surface until the finish is thoroughly softened. The surface is then padded or brushed until a fairly even film is obtained. It will level when it dries and may be rubbed down with fine steel wool, pumice, or rottenstone and oil.

Clean all surfaces with mineral spirits to remove waxes. Pads and brushes must be clean and lint-free. Work on a horizontal surface whenever possible. Alternate applications across and with the grain, making the last stroke with the grain.

If the lacquer contains stains in lower layers, pad or brush gently to prevent streaks. Overcoat the amalgamated finish with new lacquer if desired.

Linseed oil finishes can be repaired by cleaning with mineral spirits or turpentine and then with mild detergent and water. Rub down the surface with 2/0 or 3/0 steel wool. Apply warm, boiled linseed oil, one of the variations listed on page 35, or coat with shellac or varnish.

Milk paint finishes can be cleaned with lacquer thinner, denatured alcohol, or a strong solution of green soap. They should then be washed with a mild detergent or vinegar and water. If that fails, try repainting with milk paint using the formula described on page 67.

Paint or enamel finishes are usually best sanded down and recoated as described on page 47. But, if the enamel base is a lacquer, lacquer amalgamation may work.

Penetrating sealer finishes can be restored by sanding and then applying one or more coats with fine steel wool as described on page 35.

Peeling calls for finish removal, since it is caused by something interfering with topcoat adhesion and isn't likely to clean without stripping and refinishing.

Scratches may be treated as a kind of chipping, or they can be filled in with layers of liquid lacquer, varnish, or shellac. Apply such fillers with an artist's brush. If the scratch is into the wood, touch up the wood color with stain or pigment. Fine hair line scratches may be removed by polishing with pumice or rottenstone and oil, or they can be amalgamated and recoated.

Shellac finish reamalgamation is the same as lacquer finish reamalgamation, except that denatured alcohol or 3:1 alcohol-lacquer thinner is used as the solvent. Warning: moist atmosphere or water adulterated alcohol will make the amalgamated finish blush. If this should happen, reamalgamate with clean alcohol on a dry day. Apply a top coat of new shellac, then rub down.

Shellac stick patching requires practice, but it is well worth the effort. You will need a selection of shellac sticks. You will also need a can of Sterno or an alcohol lamp, a firm but flexible spatula (grapefruit knife, ground down hacksaw blade, or artist's spatula), abrasive paper, a flat, hand sanding block, and rubbing oil.

Heat the blade and shellac stick (without burning or smoking) in the clean, smokeless flame. Transfer the molten shellac to the damaged surface and butter it smoothly into place. Smooth the surface with the blade just hot enough to smooth, not bubble. Cool and shave the raised surface with a very sharp blade. Grind it flat with block-mounted, 6/0 abrasive paper, lubricated with rubbing oil. Final finish can be a French polish on shellac, varnish or lacquer surfaces, or lacquer on lacquer surfaces.

Shoe polish and colored waxes are often used for quick, temporary hiding of minor scratches. The damaged area will have to be dewaxed before refinishing. If wax enters the wood, you will have to shellac-shield it before finishing, or the wax will gum up the finish.

Varnish finish amalgamation can be approximated by rubbing with a mixture of 1:1 turpentine and boiled linseed oil, which may fill in the surface for eventual varnish overcoating. Usually stripping and refinishing is better.

Veneer chips can be repaired or replaced by the same means as those listed under INLAYS. Blistered veneer occurs when the glue lets go. If the original glue was hide glue, heating and pressing down until cool may work. Slicing the bubble with the grain to allow cleaning and injecting glue, then clamping as illustrated on page 17 may work. If these fail, remove the bubbled veneer with a thin sharp knife, and treat it as an inlay repair.

FILL CLEANED DEPRESSION with melted shellac; then smooth and level with a heated spatula.

SAND SURFACE of repaired area level with surrounding surface using 6/0 abrasive paper over wood block.

Wax finishes are hard paste wax on bare wood. To touch them up, clean with a damp rag and mineral spirits, if necessary. Apply more hard paste floor wax or automobile wax.

Wax stick patching is the quick and easy patch for burns, gouges, and scratches. However, it is not as durable as shellac stick. Wax sticks designed for patching contain blended waxes, including beeswax to produce the right consistency, but wax crayons also work well.

You will need the same equipment as for shellac stick patching: a firm, flexible blade, a smoke-free gas or alcohol flame, and a single edge razor blade.

Heat enough wax stick in a small container or spoon bowl, blend in two or more colors to match the finish, then let it cool. If the color is correct when cool, reheat and proceed; otherwise, reblend for color match. Drip the melted wax into the hole, completely filling it with a slight excess of wax. Use the knife or spatula blade to smooth the wax by compressing it with the flat side and scraping it with the dull edge.

A final touchup with the razor blade may not be necessary, depending on your skill with the spatula. Burnish the surfaces with your finger tip. If the repair is in an out of the way, wear-free spot, it can remain as it is. If it is to receive wear, coat the wax with shellac, then coat with varnish or lacquer. The shellac is a must, or the wax will foul the surface coat and cause drying and adhesion problems. For the same reason, if you insist upon level sanding the shellac, don't cut through to the wax, or the surface coat will be sticky. If your first attempt goes awry, merely dig it out and start over.

Spots on the finish usually fall into one of four categories: entirely on the surface, barely into the surface, deeply into the finish, and through the surface and into the wood. Surface spots can be the remains of almost anything spilled on the surface that doesn't penetrate or dissolve the surface. Attempt to remove the spot with a 1:1 mixture of vinegar and water. Next, try mineral spirits or turpentine. If they fail, use a mild abrasive, such as 3/0 or 4/0 steel wool, pumice or rottenstone in rubbing oil.

In-the-surface spots range from water-produced blushing to surface marring by mild solvents or abrasives.

In all cases, clean throughly with vinegar and water (1:1) and mineral spirits, then use a mild abrasive as described for surface spots. A variation on abrasives is to use white cigar ash and rub it in dry or with a little rubbing oil with a cork or felt pad, or finger tip.

Deep in-the-surface spots, if they are in the varnish, will have to be abraded and patched or stripped and completely refinished. If the surface is lacquer or shellac and if the spot is discolored, abrade through the discoloration and apply the compatible solvent (denatured alcohol for shellac and lacquer thinner for lacquer). Use a fine spray, such as an artist's air brush, a soft brush, or a soft, lint free pad. Use the brush or pad as dry as possible while transferring small quantities of solvent to the damaged area.

The purpose is to reamalgamate any undiscolored but damaged finish remaining. It may take several minutes of gentle wiping and additional solvent. When the remaining finish is satisfactorily clear, allow it to dry and patch with new lacquer or shellac. It will be necessary to rub down with steel wool, pumice, or rottenstone and rubbing oil.

If the deep spot is in shellac or lacquer and if the spot is not discolored, start the solvent treatment after thorough cleaning.

Worn edges are inevitable, if the piece was made with knife-sharp edges. Round off the edges to at least a ⅛-inch radius and refinish. If edge patching is necessary, touch up the color with stains or pigments. Any standard stain will work, if the wood is bared and will accept it. Otherwise, apply a vinyl wiping stain or thinned paint blended to match the color, with a small artist's brush. Cover the dried color with varnish, lacquer, shellac or French polish to match the original finish. Rub down as necessary to match the surrounding surfaces.

Spots through the finish and into the wood are often black or dark in color and caused by hard water reaching the wood. They require removal of the finish, then removal of the stain from the wood. Some can be removed by application of household chlorinated bleach, applied diluted or full strength and kept wet until the spot fades. If this fails, graduate to oxalic acid as described on page 24. Allow the oxalic acid to bleach the stain, then neutralize with borax solution (see page 24). Although most stains are removed by oxalic acid, a few may require the use of the commercial, two-solution bleaches.

A word of caution: the bleaches may lighten the natural or stained colors around the old spot, so unless you are good at patching colors, it might be easier to bleach the entire surface and restain the entire surface.

Brushing and Spraying

BRISTLE TIPS must be flagged (split and frayed) in order to produce the smoothest possible finish.

CHECK SPRINGINESS of brush by pressing against hand. Good bristles spread evenly, feel soft and silky.

Whether to brush or spray is a problem for many home craftsmen. Many people feel that the use of spray equipment is the only way to a quality finish. A great many craftsmen resort to a brush for critical work and use spray only where it provides maximum time advantages.

Brushes

It is a temptation to buy cheap "throw away" brushes instead of taking care of and reusing good brushes. There really is no such thing as a cheap brush. There are some that seem less expensive than others, but, ultimately, they are expensive when you consider the frustration they can cause.

The best brush you can honestly afford, properly cared for, is the cheapest brush you can buy. Barring catastrophe, good brushes last for years and improve with proper care.

Bristles are the most important part of a brush. Some workers swear by natural bristle and some by nylon bristle. Nylon far excels natural bristle for use with water base materials. Except for the greater shininess, good nylon bristles look almost like natural hog bristle: tapered shape, flagged ends, and they are just as flexible. For some special purposes, natural bristles or ox hair, sable and other materials will still dominate many art fields.

A good brush picks up, holds, and delivers ample finishing material for the job. It has flagged tips to provide smooth material flow without voids or ridges. Its bristles are tapered and of varying length to provide controlled spring and flexibility. Its bristles are also locked in place to prevent vagrant bristles from spoiling your work. Inspect each brush you buy to make sure it fits your needs. It should have bristles somewhat longer than the brush is wide.

All bristles should be tapered and flagged—any square butts of bristle automatically rule out a brush. There must be enough bristles present to do the job. Squeeze the heel of the brush (about 1-inch below the metal ferrule) to check for a skimpy, easily depressed feel. If skimpy, it indicates large wedges inserted to fool the customer into believing he has a thick brush. Small wedges are desirable for proper bristle spacing and paint holding characteristics. The tip should be wedge or chisel shaped to provide maximum bristle tip contact with the surface.

Lacquer brushes, or those used for lacquer based enamels, should be cleaned in an inexpensive lacquer thinner. When they are as free of material as possible, wash them thoroughly in warm water. Do not use hot water; hot water curls natural bristle brushes and deforms nylon. Hang the brush up to dry, bristles down. Store in its original wrapper, a heavy paper wrapping, or hang in a cool, clean, dry place.

Shellac brushes may be cleaned in denatured alcohol (shellac thinner), then washed in a warm, mild detergent solution. Or, wash them directly in warm water with household ammonia added—the foamy type is excellent. Rinse, dry, and store like the lacquer brushes.

Varnish and enamel brushes may be cleaned in inexpensive paint and varnish thinner. Switch to a good solvent-type brush cleaner for the final rinses. With pigmented material, it may be necessary to brush and comb the bristle with a steel brush or painter's brush comb to remove material in the heel of the brush.

When solvents have removed as much material as possible, wash the brush in a warm detergent solution, rinse, and dry, then rinse in turpentine. The turpentine rinse leaves natural bristles especially flexible and soft. Wrap and store the brush.

A good $4 to $5 investment is a vapor type brush conditioner which will soften a mis-used brush and greatly ease cleanup.

When you want to finish a project in the next day or so, and don't want to clean the brushes, hang them in an appropriate solvent (lacquer thinner for lacquers, denatured alcohol for shellac, and turpentine for varnishes and enamels, or the specific thinner recommended for the specific varnish or enamel in use). Avoid cheap paint thinners for brush storage, because the small amounts of thinner carried into the varnish or enamel can curdle the mix. For longer enamel or varnish wet storage, use a 2:1 mixture of raw linseed oil and turpentine, rinse in the turpentine and dry before using.

In all cases, hang the brushes in the brush keepers; don't set them on their bristles. Holes in the handles of all brushes make hanging arrangements simpler.

STORE BRUSHES in cans of vapor-type brush conditioner which can be purchased at paint supply stores.

Spraying

Spray equipment ranges from throw-away and refillable spray cans with a few ounces of finish to the many varieties of powered spray equipment.

The throw away and refillable spray cans can be extremely useful for the smaller jobs you are likely to encounter, especially for lacquer application. Investigate the several varieties of refillable spray can units. You can use virtually any material when it is properly thinned, and you can replace the propellant can as necessary.

The problem with all spray cans is that they do not have the power or wide enough spray pattern to cover very much faster than efficient brushing. Also, they generally require thinned finishing materials which take longer to color and build up thickness. On the other hand, with a little practice and proper between-use cleaning of the nozzles, tubes and jars, you can do many things that are impossible by brush. Try putting a mist coat of finish or color on with a brush—it is easy by spray

NOZZLE of spray can at left gives conical spray. Nozzle at right gives fan spray that can be rotated.

can. Feather-edge shading, stenciling, or obtaining a smooth lacquer finish are naturals for a spray can—if the job isn't too large.

Power spray equipment for home craftsmen includes the self-contained vibrator-driven gun types, the motor-driven diaphragm types with bleeder type guns, the motor driven piston and tank types with non-bleeder type guns, and the motor driven, airless sprayers.

The vibrator driven sprayers have small high speed pumps driven by a vibrator. For thin materials they perform adequately, but tend to require adjustment and, for their cost, they have an output not significantly greater than the output of a spray can.

Diaphragm type compressor units use a motor and eccentric drive to move the center of a flexible diaphragm back and forth in an enclosed space. With proper valving, the diaphragm pump can produce 30–40 psi and a volume of 2.5 cubic feet per minute, which is sufficient to drive a bleeder type gun using most finishing materials slightly thinned down.

Piston and tank spray units use a motor to drive a piston in a cylinder, much like the one cylinder engines on lawn mowers. They can, depending on driving motor power and number of pistons, supply pressures and volumes in excess of anything needed for normal finishing. A one horse power, twin piston unit can easily supply 6 cubic feet per minute at 40 psi which will handle anything you are likely to use.

Airless sprayers provide a finer control of spray patterns, less overspray, and fewer drying problems with high volatility thinners.

Spray guns are available in many variations:

Pressure feed guns employ a small portion of the air pressure to force the finishing materials from the container up to the nozzle.

Suction feed guns use a nozzle which passes the air at high velocity past the open feed tube which in effect creates a local vacuum, pulling the material up and out.

Internal mix nozzles present a smooth face and mix air and material before they leave the orifice.

External mix nozzles have two fins projecting from the circumference of the air cap and ahead of the orifice. Air is directed at the center from air holes in the fins to mix with and atomize the material. They are used with suction feed.

Nozzles providing fan-shaped patterns, 90 or 45-degree angle sprays, are available in addition to the standard conical spray pattern.

Hints

1. Instead of thinning finishes for spraying, you might consider a trick used in industry. Except for some water based materials, heating the material to about 125° F will lower its viscosity, make it spray easier and build up faster. Since most finishing materials are highly flammable, heat away from open flame or sparks. Water heated in an electric fry pan or cooker with an accurate control is ideal.

2. Spray corners first, with the spray pattern overlapping both sides of the corner.

3. Work from a finished area into an unfinished area so that overspray won't powder a finished surface.

4. Use your bleeder type gun with trigger closed (material off) as an air duster before spraying.

5. Hold the gun so that the midline of the spray is always at right angles to the surface.

6. Once you have established the gun-to-work distance for your equipment (depending on air pressure and other factors), stay with it. Moving the gun toward (runs and sags) or away (pebbly or sandy) from the surface causes trouble.

7. Never stop the gun motion. Uneven or stopped motion cause enlarged spots, runs, sags, or excess buildup.

8. *Be sure to clean gun and cup thoroughly each time you use it,* or you will regret the time wasted in restoring it. A vapor type brush conditioner does a good job of ungluing a gun that was not cleaned.

SPRAY CANS...USEFUL FOR SMALLER JOBS

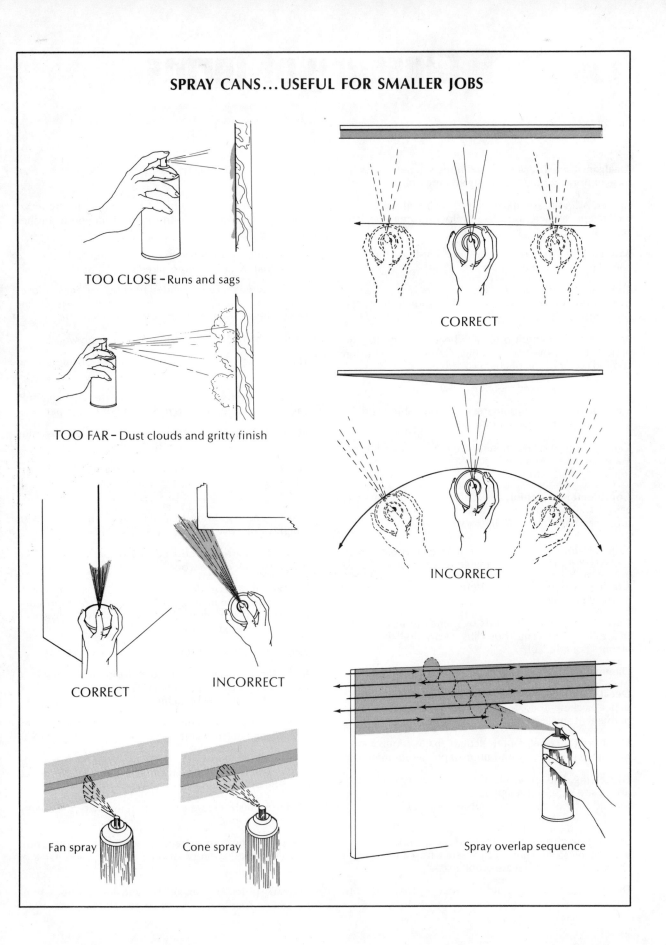

TOO CLOSE – Runs and sags

TOO FAR – Dust clouds and gritty finish

CORRECT

INCORRECT

CORRECT

INCORRECT

Fan spray

Cone spray

Spray overlap sequence

A Glossary of Terms

Amalgamation. The act of combining separate parts into a uniform whole—as amalgamating crazed shellac.

Amber. A fossil resin having a yellow-brown and translucent appearance, used in jewelry and fine specialty varnishes.

Base coat. The first coat of the final finish, or the basic color coat used under a glaze.

Bleeding. A bad habit of many stains and natural wood dyes of dissolving in solvents and spreading into adjacent finish layers.

Boiled oil. Linseed oil originally heated for prolonged periods to improve drying ability. Currently most often "boiled" by addition of chemical driers.

Bronze. Finely divided metallic powder.

Burnish. The act of producing a lustrous, shiny surface by rubbing with a firm smooth tool.

Catalytic finishes. "Hardeners" are necessary with these materials and are supplied in separate containers in liquid or powder form.

Complementary color. The color appearing directly across the standard color wheel from a given color; produces a neutral color or gray when mixed.

Copal. Natural resins from any of several tropical trees, collected from the trees or mined in fossil form.

Crazing. A fine net-like pattern of fine cracks found on aged finishes.

Cut. The number of pounds of shellac resin dissolved in a gallon of solvent. Thus 4 lbs. of dry shellac in 1 gal. alcohol is a 4-lb. cut.

Dammar. A natural resin produced in Southeast Asia.

Decal. Paint or plastic film which is obtained on a paper backing then transferred from the paper to a permanent surface.

Denatured alcohol. Grain alcohol made repulsive for human consumption by addition of poisonous materials.

Distressing. The art of selectively damaging wood or its finishes to achieve the appearance of age. Also applied to spattering of dark glaze spots on finishes.

Drier. Any of several chemical additives used to speed drying of varnishes, enamels, and paints; obtainable at most paint stores, but to be used with caution since an overdose causes severe problems.

Dutch metal. Artificial gold leaf that is produced from thin leaves of brass or bronze.

Eggshell. A finish texture very similar to lustre of an egg shell.

Epoxy. A tough, hard synthetic resin noted for its amazing adhesive powers; found in many modern finishes and glues.

FFF. Pumice powder is graded as single, double, or triple float, which is abbreviated to F, FF, or FFF.

Feathered edge. Edges sanded to subdue ridges or level differences. The blended edges between colors, or finishes where the blend is smooth and indefinite.

Firply. A handy abbreviation used for fir plywood.

Flat. A finish texture which produces absolutely no reflections.

Flint. An alternate name for the material commonly called sand when used to make sand or flint paper.

Fossil resins. Natural tree resins which are naturally aged in the ground, then mined for use.

Gesso. A smooth, workable mixture of gypsum, zinc white, and glue used as a plaster to provide a smooth surface.

Glossy. The condition of a silky, smooth surface with a highly reflective but not mirror-like finish.

Grain. The pattern produced in a wood surface by the fiber structure of the wood.

Hardwood. A term designating wood from non-coniferous (non-cone bearing) trees. Not a literal term since many so-called hardwoods are actually physically softer than those called softwoods.

Kerf. The path cut through wood by a saw blade.

Knot. Usually a darker colored inclusion in wood where the grain is at right angles to and cuts across the normal grain. The result of branching or budding in the tree.

Latex. A name commonly applied to any water based varnish, enamel, or paint.

Lubricant. Any material used between two rubbing surfaces to reduce friction or, as in sanding, to reduce clogging in the abrasive grit.

Matte. A finish texture similar in reflectivity to drawing or blotting paper.

Methyl alcohol. An extremely poisonous alcohol produced by distillation of wood, hence its trade name of wood alcohol.

Mineral spirits. Less expensive and less odorous thinner than turpentine, used for some paints and varnishes.

Nibs. Small conical projections above a finished surface caused by wet finish crawling up fiber or dust particles.

N.G.R. stain. Non-grain-raising stains, made with fast drying solvents that do not swell or raise wood grain, and are more easily handled than alcohol stains.

Oleoresinous varnish. A finishing material made of drying oils and resins or gums which hardens primarily by oxidation of the drying oils.

Opaque. Impervious to light, or, in finishing terms, any finish that blocks a view of the wood surface.

Overcoating. The process of completely coating a surface or previous finish.

Padding. The process of using a pad or wad of material to apply a finish with a wiping motion.

Pigment. Color in finely powdered form which is used to provide hue and opacity to finishes.

Polychrome finish. A finish utilizing a variety of colors.

Polyurethane. An air hardening, oil-modified urethane resin used in varnish, enamel, and paint manufacture.

Pores. Small voids or pits in wood surfaces which are actually the open ends of the tree's sap vessels.

Pumice. A volcanic rock which is used as a fine abrasive in powder form for reducing the gloss of finishes.

Quartersawn. Lumber sawn out of the log as though sawn parallel to spokes on a wheel, instead of merely slicing through the log.

Resins. Natural or synthetic materials, usually solid or semi-solid, transparent or translucent, and soluble in organic solvents but not water, which are used in finish production.

Rosin. A resin obtained by steam distillation from pine wood.

Rottenstone. A finely ground silica containing limestone used for very fine polishing. Also called tripoli.

Runs and sags. Uneven or too heavy finish application resulting in a sagged or draped ridge effect.

Sanding sealer. A very thin-bodied finishing size designed to seal wood surfaces and even out surface hardness for smooth sanding.

Sap. The life fluid of a tree, the residue of which is encountered in finishing as a gummy pitch residue around knots and streaks, especially in fir and pine.

Sap streak. Pockets or cracks containing pitch deposits which, whether hard or sticky, will interfere with finish hardening or adhesion unless shellac shielded.

Satin. A finish texture having a soft sheen like that of satin or silk material.

Saturated solution. A solution in which the liquid can dissolve no more of the material being dissolved.

Scuff. The process of roughening a too smooth surface just enough to encourage good adhesion for the fol-lowing coat, especially for varnishes. Also, to rub to-gether face-to-face as with sandpaper.

Sealer. A liquid finish material designed to selectively seal or shield the surface from excessive penetration by finishing materials.

Seedy. Any liquid finishing material that has small, un-wanted, hard granules, seeds, or particles suspended in the mixture.

Set, or Set up. That point at which a liquid finishing material is no longer workable on the surface and is just hard enough to resist airborne dust penetration. Not hard enough for contact or use.

Shield. Any material that protects a surface from penetration, softening or removal by top coats.

Size. A material designed to provide surface sealing and stiffening of fibers. In gilding it also provides the adhesive action for leaf or bronze retention.

Solvent. A liquid that will dissolve a particular material.

Stick shellac. Dry shellac resin in stick form with selected color additives to approximate standard wood and stain colors for use as a hot-melt surface patching material.

Tack rag. A tacky, varnish-impregnated piece of cheesecloth, or other lint-free material, used to wipe surfaces free of dust and debris.

Tacky. That point at which a sticky surface grabs or pulls at anything touching it, but is not readily removed from the original surface.

Thinner. Any volatile liquid compatible with, and used to reduce the consistency of, a liquid finishing material.

Tipping off. The process of smoothing out finish-wet surfaces by using just the bristle tips of a dry brush to barely skim the surface.

Top coat. That coat of finish which covers another. Usually applied to the final coat.

Undercoat. Any finishing material coat used under a final or top coat of finish. Also the process of applying an undercoat.

Urethane. One of the major synthetic varnish resins obtainable in single container air drying, in moisture curing forms, and in two-container catalytic materials.

Vehicle. The liquid or carrying portion of glazes, paints, stains, or fillers.

Veneer. A thin surface layer of wood or other material used to add durability or beauty to an otherwise unsuitable surface.

Vinyl. One of the many synthetic resins used for varnishes and paints.

Wash coat. A very thin sealing or shielding coat of any finishing material.

Wod filler. Any material useful in filling open pores of wood. Silex based paste fillers are preferred.

Index (Bold numbers are primary references)